POKÉMON GO!

POKÉMON GO!

THE ULTIMATE UNAUTHORIZED GUIDE
BY
CARA COPPERMAN

St. Martin's Griffin
New York

The editor would like to dedicate this book to Zachary and Joshua. As big readers and gamers, they are the inspiration behind this book and so much more.

This book has not been authorized or endorsed by any creator, manufacturer, distributor, or licensee of Pokémon games or toys, or any creator or developer of the Pokémon GO app.

Designed by Wooly Head Design

ISBN 978-1-250-13556-8 (trade paperback)
ISBN 978-1-250-13557-5 (e-book)

For information, address St. Martin's Press,
175 Fifth Avenue, New York, N.Y. 10010.
www.stmartins.com

Library of Congress Cataloging-in-Publication Data Available Upon Request

Our books may be purchased in bulk for promotional, educational, or business use. Please contact your local bookseller or the Macmillan Corporate and Premium Sales Department at 1-800-221-7945, extension 5442, or by e-mail at MacmillanSpecialMarkets@macmillan.com.

First St. Martin's Griffin Edition: September 2016
Printed in the United States of America.

10 9 8 7 6 5 4 3 2 1

CONTENTS

UNAUTHORIZED PLAYER'S GUIDE TO POKÉMON GO

INTRODUCTION

The summer of 2016 will always be known as the summer of Pokémon GO

July 6, 2016, began much like any other day for most people in the United States, New Zealand, and Australia, but within hours people went from casually checking their phones for messages and playing the occasional game to walking around holding out their phones and shouting excitedly. Of course, we're talking about the day Pokémon GO launched in three countries and rolled out over the next few weeks to take over the world.

Some fans had been eagerly awaiting the game for months, while it took others completely by surprise. As for me, I was hosting a family barbecue when my nephews showed up from New York City. They apologized for being late, but they had been out chasing Pokémon in Central Park and couldn't tear themselves away.

My entire family was instantly hooked, and as we walked the dog through our small suburban town in Connecticut, chasing down Pokémon, we were excited and surprised to find other people playing. We didn't realize those first few days how huge this game was becoming. We approached complete strangers to share screenshots, tips, and favorite locations, letting down our guard with each other because we instantly had all discovered something amazing together: a secret app that connected a virtual game to the real world.

———◯———

I never expected to spend my seventy-ninth birthday walking around New York City with my eighteen-year-old grandson chasing Pokémon, but it was a fun experience. I like having the app and talking to people about the game, and it's a fun way to connect with all of my grandchildren. —RSC37

———◯———

CARA COPPERMAN

As we leveled up, our batteries died, and we ate through our cellular bandwidth that first weekend, we fine-tuned the way we played to work within the limitations of the game. I carried an external battery pack and added two gigs of extra data to my cellular plan to be sure our family of four could "catch 'em all" whenever and wherever we wanted. By the end of the weekend, Pokémon GO had caught the world's attention.

The day the game launched in Tokyo must have been the day the productivity of the city dropped to a record low. Groups of salarymen in black suits would stop in the middle of the road to play, and all the while they made sure not to make eye contact with fellow Pokémon GO players. —DevOSM

Soon, everyone was talking about AR—Augmented Reality. Some hated it, saying we were all walking around like zombies, staring at our phones instead of the world in front of us. They had a point—people were walking into traffic, falling into water, and even falling off cliffs because they were watching their screens. But the zombie part? That's all wrong. When have you ever seen an excited, enthusiastic zombie? Many more people embraced the game completely, but you didn't hear as much about that part in the news because all those happy people were too busy playing the game, rather than writing about their love of it.

When I was in London, a week after it launched, I saw a grandmother and her grandson playing the game while they were buying dessert and speaking Chinese. I then proceeded to catch the Gastly that the grandson-grandmother duo was throwing Poké Balls at gleefully. —Acop42

Within the first five days of its U.S. launch, players were already spending more time on Pokémon GO than Twitter or Facebook. Pokémon's servers couldn't keep up, and the app kept crashing, often in the middle of a major catch, hatch, or battle, causing each to be lost forever. There were days servers were down for hours as the developers worked hard to keep up with demand and fix bugs, yet they continued to roll the app out as planned, spreading joy and Pokémon throughout PokéStops worldwide.

When I discovered I was living in a PokéStop, it worried me, as I didn't know exactly what sort of people and how many of them would be standing on my front step. So far I have seen a sufficient number of players outside my house, but it has yet to become overwhelming. —1AndPeggy

As time went on, bugs were fixed, and we all played on. The game has woven itself into our lifestyle in many ways with people economizing their bandwidth and battery life and continuing to figure out how to use the app in the real world. Of course, that's what all of us try to do: We stay off private property, and we respect the wishes of locations where owners ask players to use the app respectfully in accordance with local rules. We play quietly in the library. We never play at school or in houses of worship, and never while driving or riding a bike. Even if we need a little reminder now and then.

"I have been following the game through production since its appearance at E3. I downloaded it around 4 A.M. the day it launched!"
—DroptheSammer

Which brings us to the purpose of this book. Whether you're a newbie, a seasoned player looking to get to the next level, or someone in between, we've pulled together tons of tips, tricks, secrets, and hacks to level up your Pokémon GO skills and help you evolve into a master player.

The plural of Pokémon is Pokémon!

POKÉMON GO!

1

ARE YOU OUT CATCHING POKÉMON?

You most likely skipped over the app description in your rush to download it and start catching, but after playing for a while, you may stop to ask yourself: "What does it mean?" "What's all this catching, evolving, and fighting for, anyway?" And to you, we provide the answers, in the form of the app's description and introduction. Take a moment to read it now . . . We'll wait . . .

———◎———

Venusaur, Charizard, Blastoise, Pikachu, and many other Pokémon have been discovered on planet Earth!

Now's your chance to discover and capture the Pokémon all around you—so get your shoes on, step outside, and explore the world. You'll join one of three teams and battle for the prestige and ownership of Gyms with your Pokémon at your side.

Pokémon are out there, and you need to find them. As you walk around a neighborhood, your smartphone will vibrate when there's a Pokémon nearby. Take aim and throw a Poké Ball. You'll have to stay alert, or it might get away!

SEARCH FAR AND WIDE FOR POKÉMON AND ITEMS

Certain Pokémon appear near their native environment—look for water type Pokémon by lakes and oceans. Visit PokéStops, found at interesting places like museums, art installations, historical markers, and monuments, to stock up on Poké Balls and helpful items.

CATCHING, HATCHING, EVOLVING, AND MORE

As you level up, you'll be able to catch more-powerful Pokémon to complete your Pokédex. You can add to your collection by hatching Pokémon Eggs based on the distances you walk. Help your Pokémon evolve by catching many of the same kind.

TAKE ON GYM BATTLES AND DEFEND YOUR GYM

As your Charmander evolves to Charmeleon and then Charizard, you can battle together to defeat a Gym and assign your Pokémon to defend it against all comers.

It's time to get moving—your real-life adventures await!

CARA COPPERMAN

Note: This app is free-to-play and is optimized for smartphones, not tablets.

As you probably already know by now, the game uses Augmented Reality to place Pokémon characters in the real world. You can run around in the real world, get exercise, spend time with friends, explore new places, get to know your neighborhood, and become a Pokémon Trainer—a dream come true for Pokémon fans everywhere.

As you go through the real world, you pass PokéStops and Gyms and stumble upon Pokémon hanging out nearby, just waiting to be caught. Throw a Poké Ball and catch that wild Pokémon and take your battle skills to the next level: A dream come true for kids who grew up on Pokémon or anyone who wants to blur the lines between fantasy and reality.

Once you've caught your Pokémon, you can help it evolve, train it, and once you get to level 5 you can enter it in Gym Battles to defend your Gym and take over new ones. As your Pokémon grow stronger, you level up as a Trainer. You start at level 1 and with hard work, dedication, and hours of game play, you can progress all the way to level 40.

5

Top five reasons everybody who's anybody ♥s Pokémon GO

1 It's not just Pokémon, it's Pokémon IRL—In Real Life!

2 You have to go outside and explore your environment to play.

3 Catching and hatching require getting some actual exercise to succeed.

4 It's social. You can connect with people and overcome social anxiety, depression, or shyness.

5 Technologically speaking, it's the first globally accepted application that uses augmented reality, fusing virtual game play and real life. Future history books will cite this as the app that started the trend!

CARA COPPERMAN

5

Top five reasons H8ers gonna H8

1 It's a single-player game, even if hundreds of players are all around you, so it ends up being just you and your Pokémon on your screen.

2 The app requires your *phone's* full attention. It won't run in the background and it uses all your phone's major processors to work.

3 The game requires *your* full attention, too. Even in battery saver mode, you need to keep an eye on the phone so you don't miss nearby PokéStops or Gyms.

4 Meeting up with strangers and following lures can lead players into dangerous situations.

5 To play the game you need to move *and* you need to watch your phone. Doing both at once can lead to distracted walking, driving, skateboarding, bicycling, and moving in general.

Who made Pokémon GO?

Pokémon GO is a combined effort of three companies: The Pokémon Company, Nintendo, and Niantic, Inc. Niantic, the company you probably never heard of before July 2016, was actually founded in 2000 as a Google start-up. The company created the augmented reality game Ingress, where basic game play is very similar to Pokémon GO: to move in the game, you have to move in real life.

BACKSTORY

Ingress: The world around you is not what it seems.

What is it? Short version: The game that provides the basic programming that powers Pokémon GO.

The whole story: Niantic released this AR MMO LBG[*] in 2013 (android) 2014 (iOS). Through a sci-fi storyline, teams follow GPS cues and battle to capture portals at places IRL[†] (think monuments & landmarks). When a team takes a portal, it connects to others to create control fields. It's way popular with fans, though most humans had never heard of it before Pokémon GO was released.

[*] AR MMO LBG: Augmented reality massive multiplayer online location-based game.
[†] IRL: In Real Life (as opposed to online).

I love the way it brings people outside and how it crosses generations. Everyone from my grandmother to random five-year-old kids are running around and throwing Poké Balls. —Acop42

While Nintendo's stock has been very active since the launch, it's really Niantic, the developer, that did most of the work and is seeing most of the profits. The Pokémon characters brought a whole new audience to the Augmented Reality gaming world, and the Pokémon brand is gaining even more new fans as a result.

What it means for you: Ingress portals are used as PokéStops in Pokémon GO. When Ingress was released, they invited users to submit locations that would make good portals for the game. A team at Niantic reviewed the submissions and activated them in the game. That explains why there are more portals in public areas and they are more concentrated in big cities.

"Portals manifest themselves usually as public art such as statues and monuments, unique architecture, outdoor murals, historic buildings, and unique local businesses. Portals are places where human creativity and ingenuity is expressed and unexplained energy phenomena emanates."* —from the Ingress website

* https://support.ingress.com/hc/en-us/articles
  /207441797-Finding-Portals.

5 Five ways to win at Pokémon GO!

1 Rack up XP (Experience Points).

2 Get to level 40.

3 Get all 28 gold medals.

4 Get Max CP (Combat Power) for all your Pokémon.

5 Overthrow all the Gyms in your area for your team.

Medals and achievements

Catching all of the Pokémon, filling your Pokédex, creating the max evolution for each Pokémon, and racking up battle wins are achievements in themselves, but the game also lets you rack up achievements, awarding bronze, silver, and gold medals as you pass each threshold.

Medal	Description	Bronze	Silver	Gold
Jogger	Walk a specific distance	10 km	100 km	1,000km
Kanto	Register Pokémon to your Pokédex	5	50	100
Collector	Number of Pokémon captured	30	500	2000
Scientist	Number of Pokémon evolved	3	20	200
Breeder	Number of Eggs hatched	10	100	500
Backpacker	Visit PokéStops	100	1,000	2,000
Battle Girl	Gym Battle victories	10	100	1,000
Ace Trainer	Times trained at a Gym	10	100	1,000
Schoolkid	Normal type Pokémon caught	10	50	200
Black Belt	Fighting type Pokémon caught	10	50	200
Bird Keeper	Flying type Pokémon caught	10	50	200
Punk Girl	Poison type Pokémon caught	10	50	200
Ruin Maniac	Ground type Pokémon caught	10	50	200
Hiker	Rock type Pokémon caught	10	50	200
Bug Catcher	Bug type Pokémon caught	10	50	200
Hex Maniac	Ghost type Pokémon caught	10	50	200
Kindler	Fire type Pokémon caught	10	50	200
Depot Agent	Catch Steel type Pokémon	10	50	200
Swimmer	Water type Pokémon caught	10	50	200
Gardener	Grass type Pokémon caught	10	50	200
Rocker	Electric type Pokémon caught	10	50	200
Psychic	Psychic type Pokémon caught	10	50	200
Dragon Tamer	Dragon type Pokémon caught	10	50	200
Fairy Tale Girl	Fairy type Pokémon caught	10	50	200
Youngster	Catch XS Rattata	3	50	300
Fisherman	Catch big Magikarp	3	50	300
Pikachu Fan	Catching Pikachus	3	50	300

Did you know...

Everyone can catch the same Pokémon if they're in the same location, and the more players in one place, the greater the chance of catching a rare Pokémon? Playing Pokémon GO is a great way to bring people together to cooperate since players aren't competing for scarce resources. At higher levels, players pick teams, train their Pokémon, and take over Gyms if they're interested in competing, but if they aren't focused on competition, there are many other aspects of the game to focus on!

Quiz: Which gamer type are you?

Pick the one that describes you best:

Casual lurker: I play to see what the fuss is all about. I like seeing where PokéStops and Gyms are, checking out which team holds the Gyms in my neighborhood and seeing which Pokémon are nearby.

Social catcher: I play when I'm hanging out with my friends. We visit PokéStops to stock up and catch whatever we happen to find.

Collector: I play to build my Pokédex. I don't just catch Pokémon, I evolve them and max out their CP to collect all of the Pokémon at their most powerful.

Achievement Hunter: I play to rack up the achievements. I do whatever it takes to earn gold medals in every category.

Competitor: I couldn't wait to reach level 5 so I could start taking over Gyms for my team and defending them.

Warlord: My goal is to take over and hold as many Gyms as possible in my local area. If I see a Gym's prestige going down, I send my most powerful Pokémon in to defend and protect it from invaders.

Team player: I've got major team spirit. I support my teammates at Gyms and IRL to keep my team strong.

Love the background music? It was composed by Junichi Masuda who also composed the music for every major Pokémon video game leading up to Pokémon GO.

POKÉMON GO: A REAL PHONE BRAIN DRAIN

Your battery and cell data drain quickly for a reason. Pokémon GO takes advantage of all the cool features of your smartphone all at once.

GPS: the game constantly tracks and updates your location using Google Maps

Graphics Processor: The images you see on the screen are created on-the-fly, which means that the information gets sent to the phone's graphics processor and then the phone creates the image. The images update constantly as you walk, which puts a huge drain on your phone's "brain."

Camera: The camera is what gives the game its best AR feature, placing an overlay of Pokémon on top of your IRL setting. You can also use the camera to snap a photo of the Pokémon before you battle.

Brightness: Since you use the game outside, the brightness usually needs to be turned all the way up so you can see the Pokémon clearly in bright sunlight.

Sound: The music and SFX constantly play classic Pokémon sounds in the background, providing your own personal soundtrack as you walk through the real world looking for Pokémon.

Basic rules before you start playing

1

Walk with your head up and your phone down

Watch out for walls, cars, trains, people, and other stuff you may bump into. Your device will buzz when you get near something you need to catch, so you don't need to walk around with your phone in front of your face! Wearing headphones will enable you not only to hear the background music but also help you keep your eyes on the road ahead and still stay alert to the appearance of wild Pokémon nearby.

2

Stay off private property

Pokémon GO's user agreement* explicitly forbids users from entering private property without permission, giving it some cover. As for wild Pokémon who appear in the middle of the road, you can catch them just as easily from the safety of the sidewalk. Remember: In the rock-paper-scissors game of life, real-life laws beat gaming rules every time!

* https://www.nianticlabs.com/terms/pokemongo/en.

Watch your battery life

As anyone knows who has played the game for any length of time, playing Pokémon GO can really eat up your battery. And it's not surprising. The app uses the GPS, graphics processor, cellular signal, and camera and keeps your phone on its brightest setting to catch 'em all in broad daylight. But there are a few tricks to keep it from draining too quickly. Using battery saver mode in the Pokémon GO app settings.

Using battery saver mode in the Pokémon GO app settings

"When activated, turning your phone upside down will have the screen turn black, while still registering your steps toward Egg hatching and vibrating when you come within catching range of wild Pokémon. In addition, I usually keep an extra battery and mobile charging cord with me when I travel." —DroptheSammer

Battery life-saving tips

Turn on battery saver to turn your screen off while your phone is rotated 180° so that the top of the phone is facing the floor and the home button is facing the ceiling. Flipping the phone facedown does not activate the battery saver.

Put your phone in Low Power Mode. On the iPhone, go to Settings>Battery and enable Low Power Mode to temporarily turn off background processes like background app refresh and automatic updates.

Turn down your screen brightness.

Turn down your phone's volume.

Turn off the AR (Augmented Reality) setting. It uses your phone's camera to show the Pokémon you catch against the backdrop of your real life settings. To disable AR, get the Pokémon in your sites, then slide the AR toggle switch in the upper right corner of the screen to off. You'll miss out on seeing Evee perched on your dog's head, but you'll gain some extra Go time.

Disable all of your background updates in settings for apps like Facebook, Twitter, and other social media, Email, other games, news feeds, and anything else your phone checks regularly to keep you updated when you're not paying attention.

Go into the Pokémon GO menu, click settings, and disable music, sounds, and vibration.

5

Watch your cell phone bandwidth

According to wirelesshack.org*, at the app's launch it uses up around 30MB for every three-to-four hours of game play if you're not in WiFi. If you're playing for an hour a day, that's 1 GB in about three days. If you're not on an unlimited data plan, restrict your play to WiFi zones as much as possible.

Conservation tip: If you're playing in a group, switch off the app on all but one phone at a time. When you're near a Pokémon, a Gym, or a PokéStop, alert your companions to open their apps and reap the rewards!

---

* http://www.wirelesshack.org/wifi-or-cell-plan-data-usage-and -pokemon-go.html.

2

READY, SET, POKÉMON GO!

HOW TO DOWNLOAD, SET UP, AND START CATCHING

As of the game's launch, it's only available to play on iPhones and Android devices. Download it from iTunes or the Google Play store for free and start playing.

WARNING: Don't download apps or programs that claim to make Pokémon GO work on tablets or other devices. They may contain viruses, malware, or glitches that could harm your device and may try to steal your personal information.

Login with a Google account or Gmail. Don't have one? Create a Google account for free. If you're a dedicated Pokémon fan or want an account just for game play, you could sign up for a Pokémon Trainer Club account to login.

Trouble logging in? Make sure you're connected to the Internet via WiFi or cellular data. The app requires that your phone stay connected to the Internet while you are using the app, even in power saver mode. If your connections are good, your phone is probably not the issue. People around the world have caught Pokémon GO fever, and just a small fraction of players all online at once may be enough to clog up the servers. If your settings are all good, keep trying!

Remember your email and password that you signed in with. Don't count on the game keeping you logged in every time you open the app. You may also need to know them to sign in from a friend's phone if you forget yours or you run out of battery!

When you log in, Professor Willow will welcome you and teach you the basic info you need to get started.

Bio: Professor Willow

Professor Willow, Pokémon professor, Kenjo Region, specializing in Pokémon habits. He invites you to help him with his research by traveling the world collecting, training, and testing Pokémon. Eager to learn more about Pokémon families and evolution, he will gladly give you one Candy if you offer to transfer or release a Pokémon to him.

His three research assistants head up the three Pokémon GO teams. Each assistant has a different focus: Spark, leader of Team Instinct, thinks a Pokémon's character all comes from hatching and nature; Blanche, leader of Team Mystic, researches evolution and believes cool-headed, calculated analysis is the secret to any Pokémon's success; Candela, Team Valor's leader, believes training, dedication, and determination can make any Pokémon a winner. Which assistant sounds right to you? Give it some thought as you play and level up… at level 5, you'll have to join the team of one of the professor's three assistants!

Will it be Team Instinct, Team Mystic, or Team Valor?

Pick the perfect Trainer name

Maybe you're one of the lucky people who have a unique name that hasn't been taken yet, but chances are your first, second, and third choices have already been taken by now. To come up with your perfect, completely unique Trainer name combine two of the following:

1 Your favorite color

2 Your favorite Pokémon

3 Your favorite Trainer

4 Your favorite food

5 Your favorite character from a book, movie, or TV show

I decided to take up the Trainer name Godefridus, which I also use in another mobile game called Summoners War. I chose the name because it means I have a versatile, clever, analytical mind, but unfortunately I cannot direct my interest toward an undertaking for long, as I do not have the patience and practicality for systematic hard work and attention to detail. —Godefridus

Create your avatar

When Professor Willow tells you to choose a style for your adventure, you'll be able to customize your Trainer avatar. Once you're happy with the results, you're ready to go!

Not happy with your look? Change your avatar whenever you want by clicking on your avatar button in the bottom left corner of the screen, then click the three lines on the bottom right and click Customize to change your avatar's outfit or gender.

You get one chance to change your Trainer name if you don't like it, so make sure you really identify with it before you confirm your name!

For absolute beginners

When you are finally logged in, your screen will display the following:

Profile: The bottom left of the screen shows your avatar, screen name, level, and how far you have to go until you level up. Click on it to open your profile.

Menu: Click the Poké Ball to open the settings screen.

Trainer: The avatar you created.

Nearby: Up to three nearby Pokémon. Click to see the full list of Pokémon who are near you.

As you travel, Gyms and PokéStops will appear.

Gym: Where teams train and battle.

PokéStop: Where you can gather supplies such as Poké Balls, Potions, and Eggs.

What you see when you click on Profile

1 Avatar

2 Name

3 Level

4 XP needed to level up

5 Number of PokéCoins you have

6 What team you're on once you choose one

7 A list of medals and achievements you can start racking up by walking, hatching, catching, and training Pokémon. The list grows as you gain more experience, and you have the ability to earn a bronze, silver, or gold medal.

8 Journal button recapping your experience as a Trainer

Pokémon Trainer Spy Tool

The Journal button is a helpful tool for parents who want to monitor how much time kids are spending on the app and see when they're playing. Journal info can't be hacked, so kids should know if they're training Pokémon when they should be in school or doing homework, the Journal won't lie for you.

What you see when you click on Menu

1 Game settings where you can switch the sound, vibration, and battery saver settings on and off. You also can access a basic guide, get help, and report issues with the game.

2 "Tips" calls on Professor Willow to review basic game play for you.

3 Pokédex brings up a matrix of numbers with images of the Pokémon you've already battled and caught.

4 Visit the shop to spend PokéCoins and use your Defender Bonus.

Earn a Defender Bonus by defending a Gym for twenty hours. Collect the bonus from the shop to earn 10 PokéCoins and 500 Stardust for every Pokémon you have defending a Gym. You can have up to 10 Pokémon defending Gyms at one time. A shield icon will appear on the top right of the shop screen if you have an active Defender Bonus. Tap the icon to collect the bonus once it's time!

You can buy PokéCoins with real money, but with strategic game play, you'll never need to spend actual money on Poké Balls, lures, or any other items you can earn with good old-fashioned hard work and determination.

5 Pokémon gives you a view of the Pokémon you've caught. You can sort them in different ways using the button on the bottom right.

Click on a Pokémon to see its complete bio.

Click the Egg tab to see Eggs you've collected and how far you need to walk, run, bike, skate, or move with the app open to hatch each Egg.

6 The items icon takes you to a list of available items you can use such as Incense, lures, Poké Balls, camera, and more.

Congratulations! You've found a PokéStop!

A PokéStop looks like a floating blue cube. When you're right next to a PokéStop, click to open it. If you are close enough, spin the photo circle to release supplies. Pop or swipe the bubbles that appear or click the X to collect the items and add them to your inventory. Once you claim the available items, the PokéStop will turn purple for five minutes before you can visit again and claim more loot.

Don't be a space invader

Don't forget to stay out of private buildings, yards, gardens, and other spaces. Respecting private property isn't just the polite thing to do—it's the safe thing to do. Owners don't always know you're invading their space to play a game and they may mistake you for an intruder with bad intentions.

Visiting a Gym

Once you've reached level 5 you get to pick a team, then use Gyms to train your Pokémon and make them stronger, defend the Gym and add to your teams Prestige Points, or click on a Gym owned by a rival team to attempt to take it over for your team.

Not at level 5 yet? Check out the Gyms near your house and see which team has control of them by looking at the colored beacon at the top. You may find one team dominates your hometown while another may need reinforcements. Keep that in mind when it comes time to pick a team. Which will you choose—the team that's in control or the underdog?

Troubleshooting tips

CAN'T LOG IN? NOT FINDING ANY POKÉMON?

- Close out of the app then go back in.

- Are you connected via WiFi or cellular? In your phone's settings, turn on cellular data to stay connected.

- Open the main menu in the app, click on settings, and log out, then enter your username and password to log back in.

- Close out of your other apps to reduce the load on your phone's processors.

- Pokémon GO servers may be offline. Wait a while then try again or type "Pokémon Go Down" into your search bar to pull up a site that monitors server activity.

MAP NOT LOADING? GPS LOCATION UNAVAILABLE? TRY THIS

- Make sure WiFi is on, even if you're not in a WiFi zone.

- Make sure GPS and location settings are set to "on."

- Download the Google Maps app and set it to run in the background.

- Disable mock locations on the Android. This one's tricky to find and accessing it depends on the build of your phone. An online search or call to tech support will walk you through the fix.

- Reset network settings on the iPhone.

- Restart your phone.

- Delete the app then reload it and log back in. You won't lose any of your game progress.

Pokémon GO: Lures attract Pokémon and people of all ages

I'm the youth leader at a local church in Scotch Plains, so I try to keep up with current trends. This one looked like fun, so I decided to try it out. Now I play in my spare time, an hour or so a day. I enjoy sitting in my office at the church, and noticing a lure has been placed at one of the PokéStops associated with our facility, going outside, and just hanging out with folks, spending time, while we wait for more Pokémon to show up, talking about the game, and just getting to know each other. One of my favorite things about this game is how it brings people together, people who live in the same town, but may never interact otherwise. Last Wednesday I invited folks to come spend some time on the lawn in front of our church building, with some snacks and cold water, and I would put lures on the two PokéStops that are within range of the lawn. The servers didn't cooperate, and although I got out the first set of lures, we all got bumped out, and couldn't get back in, but we still had people of all ages, adult couples, people and their kids stop by, talk, and play yard games for the whole hour. —Wcpedorc

3

GOTTA CATCH 'EM ALL

Choosing your starting Pokémon

Just as in the Game Boy games, you start off with your choice of one of three Pokémon from the Kanto region: Charmander, Squirtle, and Bulbasaur. After Professor Willow goes through his introduction, he offers you a choice. Click on one to select your starter Pokémon and catch it with a Poké Ball.

If you were a fan of the handheld game, you may remember that your choice of a starter Pokémon is a big deal. On Pokémon GO, it's not a big deal at all. Here's why: in the classic game, you need the better Pokémon to start your evolution off right. In Pokémon GO, you need to collect a lot of each variety of Pokémon in order to gain enough Candy to evolve them or power them up. Candies are the currency you're looking for, and you get that by catching lots of Pokémon, no matter what they are.

Pikachu, I choose you!

Okay, it's true that it doesn't really matter which Pokémon to choose when you start, but the thrill of starting with Pikachu is too big to pass up. If you haven't picked your starter already (or if you want it so badly you're willing to start over and sign in as a new user), here's how to get Pikachu to start your collection

After Professor Willow teaches you how to catch Pokémon, he will invite you to open the map around you and get started catching Pokémon. The three starter Pokémon will appear, but don't be tempted to catch them. Just walk away. (Don't worry, they won't be insulted). The trio will despawn behind you and reappear in front of you, but don't click yet! Keep walking. Be prepared to walk at least 1,000 steps before Pikachu appears. Ignore the three starters five times in a row, and they'll bring a friend . . . Pikachu! He'll never be easier to catch than when he's offered as a starter (at least without bribing him with some Razz Berries), so throw that Poké Ball and start your game off with Pikachu!

Catching tips

If you are hitting a higher level Pokémon with regular Poké Balls, they are very likely to escape. Even if you make the perfect shot, and get the Poké Ball through the center of the circle, the Pokémon may still break free (**_sooo_** frustrating). Too many tries, and the Pokémon may get bored and run away altogether.[*]

The Battle

Throw a Poké Ball to trap a Pokémon to be able to train it and enter it in battles.

Some Pokémon are easy to catch, while others will jump, dodge, duck, and make faces at you to avoid being caught.

When you come upon a Pokémon in the wild, click on it to zoom in. Place your finger on the Poké Ball, hold it until the inner colored ring begins to shrink, then flick it toward the Pokémon to capture it. You may miss the first few times, but take aim and with some practice you can become a master!

[*] www.bustle.com/articles/172569-how-to-keep-a-pokemon-in-the
-pokeball-in-pokemon.go

Catching basics

As long as you throw the Poké Ball into the outer ring, you'll have a good chance of catching the Pokémon. The different colored rings tell you the CP level of the Pokémon, i.e.: how powerful and hard to catch the Pokémon is: green, then yellow, then red. Aim for the Pokémon's head to ensure a good catch, and watch the size of the colored ring to try to gain extra skill points.

When you're trying to catch a flying Pokémon, make sure you aim for its head, not its wings. —TennisBrandon

say cheese!

Capture the moment you met your Pokémon in the wild with a snapshot you can keep and share. Whether you discovered an Eevee sitting on a brownie at the bakery or you've caught sight of Pikachu and you need to instantly Snapchat it to your friends, take a picture for visual proof of your sighting.

TO TAKE A PHOTO OF A WILD POKÉMON

1 Click on the Pokémon to bring it up in your camera.

2 Select the camera from your backpack.

3 Tap the shutter button to snap your photo.

4 It will appear alongside your camera's photos.

Become the ultimate Trainer with a skill catch

You receive 100XP each time you capture a Pokémon and extra XP for more skilled catches.

A skill catch can help you capture the Pokémon and may reduce the risk of its breaking free once you've caught it.

Four types of Skill Catches

1 NICE: 10 XP Hit the inner ring at its largest.

2 GREAT: 50 XP Hit a half-sized inner ring.

3 EXCELLENT: 100 XP Hit the smallest inner ring.

4 CURVEBALL: 10 XP Hold the ball with your finger and spin it until it vibrates, then release it toward the inner ring—think of it as winding up for a pitch before tracing the letter J on your screen. It takes practice and skill, but once you master it, you will have a better shot at catching even the red-ringed Pokémon.

To select Power-Ups like Razz Berries (after level 8), Great Balls, and Ultra Balls (after level 11): When facing off against a rare Pokémon, select the backpack in lower right-hand side of your screen. Scroll through your items until you reach the one you want. Once selected, it will appear at the bottom center of your screen, where your Poké Ball was.

How to tame your Pokémon

Having trouble catching Pokémon above level 8? Visit a few PokéStops for a chance to catch a Razz Berry. The next time a Pokémon gives you trouble, click on the Pokémon to pull it up, then open your backpack and click on a Razz Berry. The Razz Berry will appear in place of your Poké Ball. Fling the berry to toss it to the Pokémon—don't worry, you can't miss. Pokémon are suckers for those delicious treats. One taste of a Razz Berry and the Pokémon will lose some of its fight. A Razz Berry won't help you catch the Pokémon—that still takes the same amount of skill—but it will help it stay in the ball once you've made the catch.

At level 12, you'll also start receiving Great Balls, and Ultra Balls appear once you pass level 20. These improve your ability to catch and hold the rarer Pokémon and are vital to your game play once you reach this level. If you've played other Pokémon games before, you'll recognize these superpowered Poké Balls from the first classic games Red, Blue, and Yellow. Throw them as you would a regular Poké Ball, but get the benefit of increased accuracy and power when battling high CP and rare Pokémon.

After level 9, you will start seeing Lucky Eggs. Using a Lucky Egg won't improve your catching skills, but it will double the XP for any task you complete for the next thirty minutes.

My advice for catching tough Pokémon is hitting inside the white circle. When you see that they are about to dodge or get angry, do not throw the Poké Ball until they have stopped. You can not catch them when they are dodging or making faces at you, even if you make a direct hit.
—TennisBrandon

Once you catch a Pokémon, a rectangle appears at the bottom of the screen, fitting the Pokémon into its shadow in the index. Each Pokémon is surrounded by Pokémon of the same type. The shadow fills in with a portrait of the Pokémon when you catch that Pokémon for the first time.

TIP: Loading

The white LOADING Poké Ball symbol that spins in the top left quarter of your screen indicates the game is connecting to the server. Any attempt to throw a Poké Ball to catch a Pokémon while the Loading symbol is spinning may cause the app to crash and may cause you to lose the Pokémon even if you catch it. Wait until the LOADING symbol disappears to engage a Pokémon in battle.

Sam's Razz Berry tips

- Save your Razz Berries for Pokémon with orange, yellow, or red rings that appear when you hold the Poké Ball just before throwing it, as they are harder to catch.

- Don't spend your Razz Berries as soon as you get them. You never know when you'll run into a tough opponent and need to use one.

- If you don't want to spend money—and you downright don't need to—hang around near a PokéStop to stockpile your resources. They refresh within minutes and give three to nine valuable items including Razz Berries each time.

- Go for a bike ride and find all the PokéStops near you. An hour of exercise can build up a hundred items or more and help you hatch Eggs, too!

- If you tame a Pokémon with a Razz Berry, it only lasts for one round of battle. If the Pokémon breaks out or if you miss, you'll have to toss it another Razz Berry for the next throw.

What if I want to rename my Pokémon after my cat or gym teacher?

Once you've caught a Pokémon and it's entered into the Pokédex, you can change its name.

1 Open the menu.

2 Click on Pokémon.

3 Click on the Pokémon you want to rename.

4 Click the pencil next to the name.

5 Type in the Pokémon's new name.

TRACKER HACKER

TRACKING BASICS

How does Pokémon GO know where to put all the best stuff?

Thanks to Ingress* players, the game has a huge database of cool places all over the world—photos included. Download Ingress and check out the intel map to get the inside scoop on the best basic locations.

But you don't need an Ingress map to find Pokémon wherever you go.

* https://support.ingress.com/hc/en-us/articles/207441797-Finding-Portals

Plan a Pokémon GO vacation

Looking to plan your next trip? There's nothing like visiting a major tourist destination to amp up your game play!

NYC: The Nintendo Store in Rockefeller Center is a gold mine for Pokémon GO players with multiple Gyms, PokéStops, and Pokémon to catch! Also visit Central Park, Times Square, and Washington Square Park in Greenwich Village to maximize your tracking and meet other players from around the world. A visit to the subway may reap more rewards than just traveling from one PokéStop to the next—keep an eye out for Pokémon who apparently agree that it's the most efficient way to get around the city.

San Francisco: You'll find great catches on the UC Berkeley campus, Golden Gate Park, Fisherman's Wharf, and at the San Francisco Zoo.

Los Angeles: Visit Dodger Stadium, the Hollywood Bowl, the Hollywood Walk of Fame on Hollywood Boulevard, the Huntington Library, and the Santa Monica Pier to hit each of the Pokémon-friendly environments.

Chicago: The Lincoln Park Zoo is a great free place to catch Pokémon. Visit the Bean in Millennium Park, Navy Pier for water Pokémon, and Little Italy for a good concentration of PokéStops.

London: A Zubat has been spotted flying around the London Eye Ferris wheel while Big Ben has been verified as a Gym. Visit your favorite statues and monuments like Charlie Chaplin in Leicester Square and Winston Churchill at Parliament, as well as The Museum of London, Piccadilly Circus, and Covent Garden for some great catching spots.

On the way: Airports, train stations, and other transit hubs are filled with PokéStops and Gyms. Perfect for killing time and racking up XP while you wait.

Main Attractions: Disneyworld, Disneyland, Sea World, and any large local amusement attraction is sure to have more stops than you can throw a Poké Ball at.

Central Park is the best place with Kew Gardens coming in close second. Central Park wins because everyone there is playing Pokémon GO and it becomes a social experience because either you bring your friends with you or you befriend people along the way. —Acop42

Traveling about San Francisco and Berkeley has been incredible. There are at least a dozen Gyms

Pokémon GO has already become a universal language
of sorts that gets people of all ages from all places
coming together to share tips. One high school
sophomore and his brother were in a park near their
home in Connecticut and met up with a group of kids
from a rival school. "They were walking around playing
Pokémon and they were really funny. We never would
have talked with them if it weren't for the game." His
family left soon after to go on a cross-country drive
and his parents were amazed at how well the boys
were getting along. "Honestly it was the best and most
agreeable they have been on a twenty-four hour car
trip with us and one another . . . part competition, part
discovery, part pure silliness," his mother recalls.

"I was teaching my older brother how to play—we
bonded over Pokémon," he explained. They played at
every rest stop along the way. "By the time we got to
Nisswa, Minnesota, there were kids walking all over
the little town playing the game even though usually it
is very quiet at night."

Plan a Pokémon GO staycation

Even if you have no plans to travel, you don't need to stray far from home. Based on reports of the most popular spots in the big cities, your best bet for catching and training Pokémon in your hometown will be around the following places

- Fountains
- Statues
- Monuments
- Museums
- Libraries
- Plaques
- Historical places
- Fire stations
- Police stations
- Amusement parks
- Outdoor sporting arenas
- Shopping malls

Adventureland on Long Island is actually a huge Gym. I found a lot of PokéStops and Gyms there.
—TennisBrandon

The best places I've found to play Pokémon GO are highly densely populated areas—parks, and Walmart to be exact. The strangest place I have found a Pokémon was in a bathtub. —Cornholio42089

How to tell when there's a Pokémon nearby

As you track Pokémon for your next battle, the Nearby rectangle on your main screen will show you up to three nearby Pokémon. They'll be in shadow if you've never caught one of that type before. Click the Nearby icon and a 3 × 3 grid will pop up with a list of Pokémon nearby in order of proximity to you. It won't tell you which direction, though. You'll have to walk in one direction and see how the order of nearby Pokémon shifts to track the one you're looking for.

At the game's launch, each Pokémon had up to three footprints below it, indicating how far away the Pokémon was. A glitch soon after launch gave all Pokémon three footprints. Version 1.1.0 did away with nearby footprints, but still listed the Pokémon by distance.

You'll also notice things that look like rustling leaves on your map. They are actually rustling grass, and it means a Pokémon is hiding nearby. It could pop out of hiding any minute or it could sense your presence and stay hidden until it's safely outside your radar.

Another tracker tip is to follow other players. While there were many reports of stampedes and injuries in the first days after the app released that fortunately quickly died down. Stampedes have been replaced by more civil behavior that includes

- Long-distance stalking of players who look like they know what they're doing

- Chatting up people you bump into to see what they've caught nearby

- Cluing in friends on social media when you've spotted a rare Pokémon and asking them to return the favor.

Amp up your tracking

Incense: You start the game with two pots of Incense. Its mysterious fragrance attracts Pokémon to your location. If you're planning on sitting still for a half hour, use your Incense, turn on battery saver, and rotate your phone so it's upside-down, and wait for the Pokémon to take the bait!

Lure: Place a Lure Module at a PokéStop to attract Pokémon to the area for the next thirty minutes. A lure benefits everyone who stops by. Once activated, a lure sends up hearts to attract Pokémon and other players to the location. Business owners fortunate enough to have a PokéStop at their place of business often place lures to attract players and boost business.

Lure Modules need to be used intelligently. If you're in a position where you have to stay somewhere (like the DMV) for at least half of an hour, it probably is worth placing the module. Keep in mind that those around you also benefit, so make use of this with friends. —DroptheSammer

While you do get a few Lure Modules and Incense from leveling up, getting more requires an in-app purchase.

That said, take advantage of the community aspect of Lure Modules by playing with friends and taking turns placing your lures where they'll do the most good for the most people. Use a lure or Incense along with a lucky Egg to double your XP and level up faster!

A Lure Module is different from Incense because it attracts Pokémon to the PokéStop, not just to you, so it's available to other players. It's something you do to be nice. It makes the game a lot more social. It says the username of the player who placed the Lure Module. —TennisBrandon

BEWARE!

Always use common sense when following lures. Only follow lures placed in well-lit, populated areas. Never visit a lure in a dark, deserted area, especially at night or in an unfamiliar place.

But Wait, There's More!

The Pokémon GO Plus wrist tracker lets you keep your phone in your pocket while you track Pokémon around town. It connects to your phone using Bluetooth and will flash and vibrate when a Pokémon or PokéStop are nearby. Press the button on the device to begin a battle or collect PokéStop items.

- The plus: keep your phone in your pocket and let the tracker do the work

- The minus: It costs $34.99 (£34.99) and uses Bluetooth, which is an additional battery drain

The Pokémon storage upgrade lets you keep catching Pokémon even after you fill all 250 slots in your inventory. While you could transfer extra Pokémon to Professor Willow for the price of 1 candy, if you're intent on catching and keeping as many as you can, you can purchase a storage upgrade from the shop for 200 PokéCoins.

I honestly can say that the only part of the game that I don't like is the economy. The many uses of the PokéCoins vs. how to get them creates economic disparity. —Cornholio42089

Don't just track 'em, hatch 'em!

PokéStops give out more than free Poké Balls. You can also receive Eggs, which will hatch into Pokémon under two conditions

1   Place the Egg in an Incubator.

2   Walk the distance required by the Egg.

There are three types of Eggs: 2km, 5km, and 10km. The longer you have to walk, the rarer and more powerful the Pokémon you will hatch.

Distance conversion refresher course (in case you don't remember your miles to kilometers conversion rate)

2km = 1.25 miles

5km = 3.1 miles

10km = 6.3 miles

You have space for up to nine Eggs in your inventory. If you receive any more, you won't be able to place them in your inventory, so keep your Eggs incubating and hatching so you don't miss out.

Eggs also give you lots of XP, Stardust, and Candies when they hatch, which is even more incentive to get moving and hatch those eggs!

Eggs are a constant thought you need to have, and the battery saver setting can really help with this. Eggs give a lot of free Candies, and thus are very crucial for getting evolved Pokémon. I would advise you to be hatching as many Eggs as you can as often as you can. —DroptheSammer

To hatch an Egg

1 Click the Poké Ball main menu.

2 Click Pokémon.

3 Click on the Eggs tab.

4 Place the Egg in an Incubator. You'll start the game with an infinite use Incubator and will be awarded 3-use Incubators as you level up. Use the infinite use Incubator for shorter distance Eggs so you can use it more often, and use the limited use Incubators for long distance Eggs.

5 The Incubator will count down the distance you have to go before your Egg hatches.

6 When you've reached the full distance, your device will buzz and you can watch the hatching sequence to see which Pokémon pops out and how many rewards you get.

TIP: Stepping out

The app uses your phone's GPS and your phone's pedometer to track steps. You need to keep the app open (preferably on battery saver mode) as you travel to register your steps and hatch your Egg. **Steps only count when the app is open.** Set the app to power saver mode and keep the phone upside down to keep earning steps as you travel.

Stuck in slow traffic? Your app may register your distance when you're traveling at low speeds.

Always keep an Egg incubating in your infinite use Incubator!

DroptheSammer's Poké Ball conservation tips

For stockpiling enough Poké Balls

If you don't want to spend money—and you downright don't need to—hang around near a PokéStop or two. They refresh pretty quickly—within just minutes—and give valuable items three to nine at a time.

Things to do if you're running out of Poké Balls

This depends on your priorities. As a general rule, conserve. If you're out to evolve a Pokémon, focus on that. If you're out to catch 'em all, don't waste balls on repeats. Be smart about what you have at your disposal.

What to do if you didn't read the list in time and you ran out of Poké Balls anyway

The remedy is simple—if you don't want to spend money on buying them yourself, just hang around a PokéStop or go for a ride and find all the PokéStops near you. An hour can build up a hundred Poké Balls or more.

Not to mention the fact that after level 12, more balls become available (Great balls, Ultra balls, etc.) and the odds change just a little.

5

POKÉMON TYPES AND WHERE TO FIND THEM

Looking to fill your Pokédex but not sure where to find them?

The game splits the real world into biomes like park, road, monument, and other categories. The game then assigns each type of Pokémon to different habitats, making them more likely to show up in some places than in others.

There are 18 different types of Pokémon but Dark type are not available in Pokémon GO. The type relates to where they're found and their battle moves, so every Pokémon can belong to one or two types at the same time. Tentacruel is a water type and a poison type, for example, and Spearow is both normal and flying.

In the game, there are 142 original Pokémon available to catch and/or evolve. The Pokémon found in the game at its launch in July 2016 all come from the Kanto region of the Pokémon world.

As of the initial launch of Pokémon GO, only Kanto Pokémon and no Dark Pokémon are available but the company has plans to expand its Pokédex to other regions. In addition, no legendary Pokémon are currently catchable, which means you won't be catching Mew, Mewtwo, or the three team mascots, Articuno, Moltres, and Zapdos. Ditto is also not available to catch or hatch in the game.

———————◎———————

I had a picnic at the beach and my friend and I ran around the beach the whole time looking for Pokémon. They were everywhere. Every five minutes we ran to a PokéStop at a rock to collect more Poké Balls because we ran out.
—TennisBrandon

Seventeen types of Pokémon . . . plus one?

Normal: Normal Pokémon can be found everywhere. Even your living room.

- Chansey, Dodrio, Doduo, Eevee, Fearow, Jigglypuff, Lickitung, Meowth, Persian, Pidgeot, Pidgeotto, Pidgey, Porygon, Raticate, Rattata, Snorlax, Spearow, and Wigglytuff

- Farfetch'd can only be found in the wild in Asia but can be hatched from a 5K Egg anywhere in the world.

- Kangaskhan is available in Australia and New Zealand only in the wild, but it's hatchable from a 5K Egg everywhere else.

- Tauros is available in North America in the wild and can hatch from a 5K Egg in all locations.

- Ditto has not been seen in the game as of its launch date.

Fire: Fire Pokémon hang out in dry climates and neighborhoods and on the hot sand at the beach

- Arcanine, Charizard, Charmander, Charmeleon, Flareon, Growlithe, Magmar, Ninetales, Ponyta, Rapidash, and Vulpix

- Team Leader Moltres can't be found hanging out anywhere waiting to be caught as of the game's launch.

Fighting: Sports arenas, gyms, stadiums, and other competitive places

- Hitmonchan, Hitmonlee, Machamp, Machoke, Machop, Mankey, Poliwrath, and Primeape

Water: Lakes, ponds, beaches, boat docks

- Blastoise, Cloyster, Dewgong, Goldeen, Golduck, Gyarados, Horsea, Kabuto, Kabutops, Kingler, Krabby, Lapras, Magikarp, Omanyte, Omastar, Poliwag, Poliwhirl, Poliwrath, Psyduck, Seadra, Seaking, Seel, Shellder, Slowbro, Slowpoke, Squirtle, Starmie, Staryu, Tentacool, Tentacruel, Vaporeon, and Wartortle

Flying: Farmland, woods, parks, playgrounds, hiking trails, forests

- Aerodactyl, Articuno, Butterfree, Charizard, Dodrio, Doduo, Dragonite, Fearow, Golbat, Gyarados, Moltres, Pidgeot, Pidgeotto, Pidgey, Scyther, Spearow, Zapdos, and Zubat

- Farfetch'd is hatchable from a 5K Egg and available in Asia in the wild.

Grass: Farms, parks, golf courses, playgrounds, campgrounds

- Bellsprout, Bulbasaur, Exeggcute, Exeggutor, Gloom, Ivysaur, Oddish, Paras, Parasect, Tangela, Venusaur, Victreebell, Vileplume, and Weepinbell

Poison: Grass, water, power plants, industrial areas, swamps, and wetlands

- Arbok, Beedrill, Bellsprout, Bulbasaur, Ekans, Gastly, Gengar, Gloom, Golbat, Grimer, Haunter, Ivysaur, Kakuna, Koffing, Muk, Nidoking, Nidoqueen, Nidoran (Female), Nidoran (Male), Nidorina, Nidorino, Oddish, Tentacool, Tentacruel, Venomoth, Venonat, Venusaur, Victreebel, Vileplume, Weedle, Weepinbell, Weezing, and Zubat

Electric: Concrete covered areas such as schools, universities, big buildings

- Electabuzz, Electrode, Jolteon, Magnemite, Magneton, Pikachu, Raichu, Voltorb, and Zapdos

Ground: Dirt, beaches, transportation hubs, parking garages, mud, roads, and cities

- Cubone, Diglett, Dugtrio, Geodude, Golem, Graveler, Marowak, Nidoking, Nidoqueen, Onix, Rhydon, Rhyhorn, Sandshrew, and Sandslash

Psychic: Beaches, playgrounds, forests, parks, hospitals

- Abra, Alakazam, Drowzee, Exeggcute, Exeggutor, Hypno, Jynx, Kadabra, Slowbro, and Slowpoke

- Mew and Mewtwo are not available in the game as of launch.

- Mr. Mime is a regional Pokémon only available to catch in the wild in Europe, but can be hatched worldwide from a 10K Egg.

Rock: Pavement, street, gravel, malls, large buildings, town centers

Aerodactyl, Geodude, Golem, Graveler, Kabuto, Kabutops, Omanyte, Omastar, Onix, Rhydon, and Rhyhorn

Ice: Water, snow, grassy areas

Articuno, Cloyster, Dewgong, Jynx, and Lapras

Bug: Playgrounds, grass, gardens, paths, nature preserves, hikes

Beedrill, Butterfree, Caterpie, Kakuna, Metapod, Paras, Parasect, Pinsir, Scyther, Venomoth, Venonat, and Weedle

Dragon: Landmarks, monuments, and famous places

Dragonair, Dragonite, and Dratini

Dark: No Dark Pokémon are available

Ghost: Dark places, at night, churches, parking lots

● Gastly, Gengar, and Haunter

Steel: Train stations, inside large buildings, near train tracks

● Magnemite and Magneton

Fairy: Landmarks, monuments, churches, and cemeteries

● Clefable, Clefairy, Jigglypuff, and Wigglytuff

● Mr. Mime is available regionally or by hatching.

As I go to different places I am always sure to play Pokémon GO . . . When you are far from home you can find many Pokémon that you wouldn't typically find walking down the street in your hometown.
—1AndPeggy

CARA COPPERMAN

6

GET UP, GET OUT, AND POKÉMON GO

One major reason parents and teachers hate video games is that they encourage gamers to stay indoors and keep them from getting exercise. Motion-activated games like Xbox One Kinect and WiiU get you moving but keep you inside while apps and portable game devices like the 3DS and the PlayStation Vita get you outdoors but tied to the game.

Pokémon GO may still ruffle a lot of adult feathers, but one thing the game does is get gamers moving outdoors in the real world and gets people interacting with each other. In the first week of launch, gamers around the globe were already reporting the health benefits of the game.

Remind all players, young and old, to be aware of their surroundings when they play and never venture alone into unfamiliar territory, especially at night.

How Pokémon GO secretly gets you moving

Walk to hatch: You'll need to travel from one and a quarter miles to just over six miles to hatch each Egg.

Walk to catch: You can play from your living room, but unless your house doubles as a PokéStop or Gym, gameplay will be limited to catching the occasional indoor Zubat and Rattata, trading extras with Professor Willow, and evolving your Pokémon. You'll need to get outside to really experience the game.

Venture out to expand your Pokédex: If you stay in one place, you're limiting yourself to one type of Pokémon for that area. Venturing out to new places helps you fill in the blank spaces in your Pokédex.

What you'll gain from being a dedicated gamer

Discovering your neighborhood: Exploring your neighborhood to expand your Pokédex and resources introduces you to new places you don't usually visit.

Serendipity: Exploring on vacation gives you a destination and goals. As you search for Pokémon, you'll come across unexpected pleasant surprises.

Serendipity (ser·en·dip·i·ty /ˌserənˈdipətē/) (noun): A happy accident. Finding a pleasant surprise when you are looking for something else.

Exercise: Walking as you game burns calories, helps your heart, moves your muscles, boosts your energy levels and your mood, and may even help you do better on tests by helping your brain remember things better.

Interaction: As you travel the world in search of new Pokémon to train and new Gyms to dominate, you will find people are more friendly when they find you're both after the same rare Pokémon. While the people you meet probably won't become your new best friends, the game is giving people a sense of community and belonging that most games don't have.

While at the end of the day, it's just your Trainer avatar and the Pokémon you train on your screen, playing means you're still connecting IRL with actual human beings, which has a much bigger benefit than online gaming and chats where you probably never meet your opponents or teammates.

Family time: Pokémon GO is simple enough for a little kid to play, challenging enough for adults, and complex enough for people of all ages and interests to get something out of playing. It's become a great family activity for vacations, day trips, hikes, and even running errands. Many families report they head outside to catch Pokémon instead of watching TV as a family in the evening.

> *Our kids' bedtime routine has really been transformed by the game. Gone are the DVDs we've seen so many times we've memorized them. We're now heading out to catch Pokémon instead. Our dog gets a lot more exercise, we catch more Drowzee and Clefairy Pokémon since it's late in the day and our son sleeps more soundly, too. We get to hang out and talk about things with our kids on a whole new level now that we have Pokémon GO as our common ground. It's really brought us together.*
> —*Jacqueline, mom of two kids in Connecticut*

One fifteen-year-old gamer was stuck in the airport on his way home from camp with only $1 in his pocket. "I was totally by myself. I was hungry and alone and all I wanted to do was to get home to my family." Fortunately, the airline handed out $25 food vouchers to the stranded passengers, so he set off in search of food. On his way to the food court, his phone buzzed, indicating a Pokémon nearby. As he caught it, he saw another teen tossing a Poké Ball to catch the same one. They teamed up and spent the rest of the evening visiting the PokéStops and Gyms in the terminal and catching Pokémon. "By the time we finally boarded the plane seven hours later, our group had expanded to include two nine-year-old kids and a security guard, and we had each caught about 25 Pokémon," he recalled. "Pokémon GO made what could have been the worst night of my life a pretty fun experience!"

My favorite thing about this game compared to the other Pokémon games is that it makes me want to go outside and walk around and meet new friends. It's certainly been a positive influence so far.
—Godefridus

Pokémon GO and your health

The game is still relatively new, but doctors and psychologists are already talking about the many benefits of the game.

Soaking up sunlight as you walk around outdoors playing the game can help in the fight against seasonal mood disorders, depression, and anxiety.

I'm sure I'll play a bit less once I've caught all I can, but it's still fun to just leave the house and see what pops up. Plus, it's good exercise and I might see some real Pokémon—BIRDS!—while outside!
—Commander Holly

There are some drawbacks as well. Some opponents of the game are disappointed there are no accessibility options for players who are visually impaired or are unable to tap and swipe, although modifications may come with later builds. And the news is filled with stories of players who forget to watch where they're going and don't use their best judgment and walk into traffic, bump into parked cars, and unwittingly head into dangerous areas with disastrous results. Not to mention players who play the game while driving, biking, or skateboarding who can cause injuries to themselves or others. To combat these hazards, it's safer and more fun to play as a team with friends. The added benefit: saved battery and cell data usage. When you play with friends, only one person needs to keep the app open at all times as they can alert the rest of the players when there's something to catch in the game.

Heading outside to play?
Don't forget sun protection!

Online groups, like Facebook, let you share information, and also know when people will be out hunting, or placing lures. —Wcpedorc

7

EVOLVE! POWER-UP WITH CANDY!

(AKA "WHAT TO DO WHEN YOU HAVE TOO MANY VENONATS IN YOUR POKÉDEX")

Evolution facts

Not all Pokémon are created equal. In all of the Pokémon games, evolution plays a huge part in gaming and strategy. Evolving Pokémon makes them stronger and gives them better skills.

You may find, as you walk through the game, you're catching a whole lot of Weedles—they look a little like a worm in a party hat. This poisonous bug may not look threatening, but catch enough Weedles and you'll accumulate 12 Candies to evolve it into Kakuna (who looks like a worm with a necktie). 50 Kakuna Candies later, and you'll have enough to evolve a Beedrill, who deals 6 damage with each bug bite attack and 15 damage for each poison jab. Beedrill also has some pretty fresh specialty moves that deal 25 to 50 damage, but more on that when we talk about combat later.

Kakuna and Beedrill are each available to catch in the wild as well, but they are harder to catch and not as readily available. Some Pokémon are only available through evolution.

Confused about which Pokémon evolve and what they become? Click on the Poké Ball menu, then click on your Pokédex to open it. Select the any Pokémon you've already caught to see how it evolves and what stage it is in its evolution. A number in place of a Pokémon indicates you haven't caught that Pokémon yet. Check the Appendix A at the back of this book for a complete list of Pokémon available to catch at the release of the game.

Why does the game keep giving me Candy?

When you capture a Pokémon, you receive Candy specific to that Pokémon. Also, each Egg you hatch will give you anywhere from 3 to 35 Candies for that type of Pokémon.

TIP: Eggs vs. Candy

Hatching Eggs is a great way to get Candy for otherwise rare Pokémon.

The Candy type is specific to the basic, unevolved level of Pokémon as well as its leveled-up versions. You receive Weedle Candy for catching or hatching a Weedle, a Kakuna, or a Beedrill.

I'm excited to have a Beedrill, which is the evolved form of Kakuna, which evolves from Weedle. It takes a number of Candies to evolve, but can be worth the grind to get a higher CP bug Pokémon early on. —DroptheSammer

TIP : Power-Up before you evolve

Start with a weak Pokémon, a weak Pokémon will evolve at the next level. Evolve a Pokémon with high CP to get a stronger next-level version of the species. Evolve your highest CP of a species and trade off the lowest. Check out the chapter on Power-Ups using Stardust and Candy to learn how to strengthen your starting Pokémon to end up with a higher CP product of evolution.

Meat grinder strategy

One way to upgrade your common Pokémon quickly is to harvest as many of the low-level Weedle, Caterpie, Pidgey, Rattata, Female Nidoran, Male Nidoran, Zubat, and Venonat Pokémon as you can while you're on a low level. When you think you have a good handful of these minions, check your Pokémon inventory. You may have enough to trade in your Candies to evolve some of them into more powerful players.

To check to see if you have enough for an evolution

1 Click the Poké Ball in the bottom center of your screen to pull up the menu.

2 Click the Pokémon icon on the bottom left.

3 Click the Pokémon you want to evolve. Make sure it's the Pokémon with the highest CP of its type. It will keep the same CP when you evolve it. Evolving a 10CP Pidgey gives you a low CP Pidgeotto, but a 126CP Pidgey starts its evolved life off in a better place as a Pidgeotto with more CP of its own.

4 Below the Pokémon's stats that tell you the type of Pokémon and its dimensions, you'll see how many candies you have for that specific Pokémon.

5 At the bottom of the screen by the X, you'll see the word Evolve. If Evolve is grayed out, you don't have enough Candies to evolve the Pokémon just yet. The Candy icon and number tell you how many you need to complete an evolution.

6 If you do have enough Candies, click Evolve. A pop-up will ask if you want to evolve your Pokémon.

7 Click YES.

You'll find that some Pokémon you've caught don't have the Evolve button. That's because they are at the top of the Evolution chain for that type. They cannot evolve any further.

TIP : Worth the Fight?

Some hard-to-catch Pokémon just aren't worth the fight. A Zubat, for instance, can be pretty tricky to catch starting at the earlier levels. Since evolving a Zubat requires 50 Candies, unless you're desperate to evolve a Zubat into a Golbat to fill every spot in your Pokédex, it may not be worth the wasted Poké Balls unless you have unlimited access to Poké Balls by living or working at a PokéStop.

Transferring

If you almost have enough of one type of Candy, you can transfer some of your spare Pokémon to Professor Willow for one Candy of that type. You'll want to trade your Pokémon with the LOWEST CP since you'll get the same amount of Candy whether you're giving him a 10CP Pidgey or one with 126CP.

To transfer a Pokémon to Professor Willow for one Candy

1 Click the Poké Ball to open the main menu.

2 Click on Pokémon on the bottom left.

3 Click on the Pokémon with the lowest CP of the type you want to transfer.

4 Scroll all the way to the bottom of the screen and click Transfer.

5 You will be reminded that you can't take your Pokémon back once you've transferred it. Press Yes to continue.

6 A message will appear that the transfer has succeeded. You have received one piece of Candy specific to that Pokémon.

> *I trade dozens of times every single day with the professor. I turn in all duplicate Pokémon and all the un-evolved versions that I already have the evolved version of, because it yields CP and in-game consumables. —Cornholio42089*

Even when you have a max evolution version of a Pokémon, you can still keep catching and grinding low-level Pokémon to evolve them for the XP bonus alone.

Reasons to evolve Pokémon

- You get new Pokémon in your Pokédex you haven't caught before.

- You get 1000 XP the first time you evolve a Pokémon species and 500 XP for every evolution after that.

- You free up space in your inventory. You only have room for 250 Pokémon, and that fills up pretty quickly.

- You have a better army of more powerful Pokémon for when you're ready to fight.

TIP: The Right stuff

Each Pokémon and its evolved forms use its own Candy. You can't evolve a Pidgey with Weedle Candy.

Bonus trick: Pair a batch of evolutions with a lucky Egg to double the XP you earn from every evolution. Keep an eye on your Eggs as they incubate. Activate a lucky Egg to double the points you get when they hatch to level up even faster!

You can evolve up to around 60 Pokémon with one Lucky Egg and you want to do that as much as possible if you want to level up. I like to always save up to around 200 Pidgey and Weedle Candy before I pop a Lucky Egg and evolve them.
—Godefridus

> *I evolve Pokémon like Rattata, or Pidgeys to gain XP. I will evolve Pokémon that I want to keep, and use, based on how strong they are at the current level. —Wcpedorc*

Evolving Eevee

You probably have caught more than you think you need of that cute furry little creature, but there's more to Eevee than meets the eye. If you're a fan of the original game, you know that Eevee can evolve into several different creatures. The evolution is complicated but predictable and is based on time of day, the use of special items, Eevee's happiness level, and available moves. In Pokémon GO, however, you'll just have to wait and see what happens after you feed it 25 Candies. Unless, that is, you know the secret to controlling your Eevee evolution.

At launch, it's only possible to evolve Eevee into the three original evolutions from the Kanto region: Flareon, Jolteon, and Vaporeon. Eevee's other five evolutions aren't available.

The Eevee Evolution Secret

Normally, renaming your Pokémon doesn't do anything but give you another reason to get the giggles every time you pull up a picture of your captured Mankey and it has your brother's name. Rename an Eevee one of three names and you can control its destiny.

- Rename as Rainer to evolve into Vaporeon

- Rename as Sparky to evolve into Jolteon

- Rename as Pyro to evolve into Flareon

Before you click Evolve, however, close out of the game and go back in to make sure the name stuck.

But WHY? You may ask. That is an excellent question and one you should be asking. Nothing in Pokémon happens quite by accident. Here's the backstory from CharmanderinMC

In the Pokémon anime, there were four brothers—Mikey who had a regular Eevee, and the other three who had the other special evolved ones. They were pushing Mikey to evolve his Eevee—but he kept his as Eevee. To evolve your Eevee the way Mikey's brothers did, select the Eevee you are evolving and rename it after one of the three brothers. I named my best Eevee Sparky and it's now Jolteon.

Evolution chart

Pokémon and Candies needed →	Evolution 1 →	Evolution 2
Bulbasaur: 25 →	Ivysaur: 100 →	Venusaur
Charmander: 25 →	Charmeleon: 100 →	Charizard
Squirtle: 25 →	Wartortle: 100 →	Blastoise
Caterpie: 12 →	Metapod: 50 →	Butterfree
Weedle: 12 →	Kakuna: 50 →	Beedrill
Pidgey: 12 →	Pidgeotto: 50 →	Pidgeot
Rattata: 25 →	Raticate	
Spearow: 50 →	Fearow	
Ekans: 50 →	Arbok	
Pikachu: 50 →	Raichu	
Sandshrew: 50 →	Sandslash	
Nidorana: 25 →	Nidorina: 100 →	Nidoqueen
Nidorana: 25 →	Nidorino: 100 →	Nidoking
Clefairy: 50 →	Clefable	
Vulpix: 50 →	Ninetales	

Jigglypuff: 50	→	Wigglytuff		
Zubat: 50	→	Golbat		
Oddish: 25	→	Gloom: 100	→	Vileplume
Paras: 50	→	Parasect		
Venonat: 50	→	Venomoth		
Diglett: 50	→	Dugtrio		
Meowth: 50	→	Persian		
Psyduck: 50	→	Golduck		
Mankey: 50	→	Primeape		
Growlithe: 50	→	Arcanine		
Poliwag: 25	→	Poliwhirl: 100	→	Poliwrath
Abra: 25	→	Kadabra: 100	→	Alakazam
Machop: 25	→	Machoke: 100	→	Machamp
Bellsprout: 25	→	Weepinbell: 100	→	Victreebel
Tentacool: 50	→	Tentacruel		

Geodude: 25	→	Graveler: 100	→	Golem
Ponyta: 50	→	Rapidash		
Slowpoke: 50	→	Slowbro		
Magnemite: 50	→	Magneton		
Doduo: 50	→	Dodrio		
Seel: 50	→	Dewgong		
Grimer: 50	→	Muk		
Shellder: 50	→	Cloyster		
Gastly: 25	→	Haunter: 100	→	Gengar
Drowzee: 50	→	Hypno		
Krabby: 50	→	Kingler		
Voltorb: 50	→	Electrode		
Exeggcute: 50	→	Exeggutor		
Cubone: 50	→	Marowak		

Koffing: 50	→	Weezing			
Rhyhorn: 59	→	Rhydon			
Horsea: 50	→	Seadra			
Goldeen: 50	→	Seaking			
Staryu: 50	→	Starmie			
Magikarp: 400	→	Gyarados			
Eevee: 25	→	Vaporeon, Jolteon, Flareon			
Omanyte: 50	→	Omastar			
Kabuto: 50	→	Kabutops			
Dratini: 25	→	Dragonair: 100	→	Dragonite

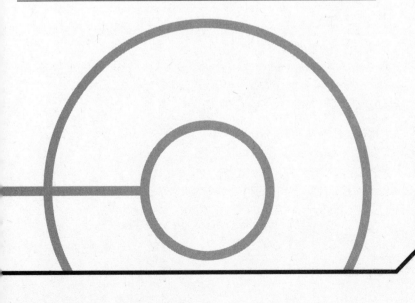

Evolution tips

Evolution is not penalizing and is Pokémon specific. If you catch an excess of Pidgeys, which I recommend you do for the extra Stardust, you may evolve them into Pidgeottos to save both space and generate a large amount of experience. Save some Candies for your strongest Pokémon to Power-Up their CP once you start attacking and defending Gyms. —Godefridus

8

PICK YOUR TEAM

When you get to level 5, Professor Willow commands you to pick your team. That team will stick with you for the life of your account. You will battle alongside these teammates, capture Gyms, create alliances, and pledge allegiance to your team leader, and you can't change your mind once you've made your choice unless you delete your account and start over.

In agony over which team to choose? Take this quick quiz to find out where you belong.

QUIZ: WHAT'S THE RIGHT TEAM FOR YOU?

When you're not playing Pokémon GO, you can be found

1 Taking things apart to see how they work

2 Playing a team sport

3 Daydreaming

What's your favorite school subject?

1 Science

2 Phys Ed

3 Writing

What's your favorite season?

1 Winter

2 Summer

3 Spring

You just picked up a novel. What's it about?

1 A futuristic adventure set in outer space

2 A tale of an athlete who trains hard to succeed against all odds

3 One person's journey to discover love, friendship, and happiness

How'd you do?

If your answers were...

Mostly 1, you should join Team Mystic

Mostly 2, welcome to Team Valor

Mostly 3, believe in Team Instinct

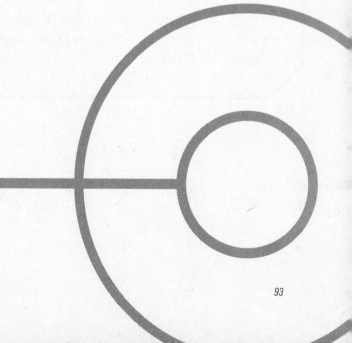

About the teams

Team Mystic: Led by Blanche, the blue team is all about the brains and the science behind Pokémon evolution when it comes to Pokémon battles. Blanche's favorite saying: *"With our calm analysis of every situation, we can't lose!"*

Team Valor: Candela leads the red team. She believes team spirit, training, and discipline are the keys to winning and keeping control of a Gym. Candela has been heard to boast: *"There's no doubt that the Pokémon our team have trained are the strongest in battle!"*

Team Instinct: Spark embraces the yellow spark of electricity. Intuition and the innate talents of each Pokémon are what makes her team's approach unique. Team Instinct's motto: *"You never lose when you trust your instinct!"*

As one of the first to play the game, there wasn't as much of a following around the teams when I reached level 5, so I made my choice based off of the description the game offered. Team Mystic is the equivalent of Harry Potter's Ravenclaw house, the group more focused on a scientific or logical approach, versus Team Valor's focus on pure power, and Instinct's dabbling somewhere in between. —DroptheSammer, Team Mystic

I checked the map and there were a lot of red gyms. It looked like the most popular and the strongest team in the area.
—TennisBrandon, Team Valor

Each Pokémon has its strengths and weaknesses, and when you're playing the classic game that's what counts. Since you don't get a chance to fight or train before you pick your team, I guess I just followed my instinct and figured that's how it would work in Pokémon GO.
—TriciaMacMillan, Team Instinct

Each team also has one of three legendary winged mirages as its mascot. Zapdos, the electric lightning-powered Pokémon, for Instinct, Articuno, who has the power to freeze things, for Mystic, and Moltres, who can melt just about anything with its fire power, for Valor.

Articuno: Artic sounds like Arctic.
Uno is the Spanish word for one

Zapdos: Zap is the sound of lightning.
Dos is the Spanish word for two

Moltres: Molt is short for molten (as in lava) or similar to melt. Tres is the Spanish word for three

But mascots, team leaders, colors, and personality tests aside, you probably just want to join the same team as your friends or family so you can battle side by side, join together to take down Gyms held by rival teams, and revel in your team spirit together. It's a social game, after all!

Up for some friendly rivalry instead? Choose sides among family and friends then battle it out to earn bragging rights and team honor.

9

LEVEL UP! TIPS AND TRICKS TO BE THE BEST TRAINER YOU CAN BE

Where the Pokémon card game focuses on leveling up your Pokémon characters, Pokémon GO is about increasing your level as a player and a Trainer. The more XP you get, the higher your level. With a higher level, you can catch rarer Pokémon and make the ones you catch more powerful. Higher level Pokémon are also harder to catch! It's important to remember that luck plays a huge role, too.

Have you noticed that Pokémon caught at the same time don't always have the same CP? A catch at a higher level earns you a Pokémon with more combat power.

It's more of a priority to level up your Trainer because every time you level, your Pokémon's CP cap rises until you hit level 30. The first thing I tell new players is to save their Lucky Eggs and Candies until they've saved enough for thirty minutes of non-stop evolution. Trainer level takes priority over everything else if you plan on being competitive with the game. Otherwise, if you just want to be a casual player, just enjoy it. —Godefridus

---

CHART OF LEVELS, REQUIREMENTS, REWARDS, AND UNLOCKS

LEVEL	XP NEEDED	TOTAL XP	REWARD	UNLOCKS
1	0	0		
2	1,000	1,000	15 Poké Balls	
3	2,000	3,000	15 Poké Balls	
4	3,000	6,000	15 Poké Balls	
5	4,000	10,000	10 Potions, 1 Incense, 10 Revives	Choosing a team, Gyms, Great Potions, Revives
6	5,000	15,000	15 Poké Balls, 10 Potions, 10 Revives, 1 Egg Incubator	
7	6,000	21,000	15 Poké Balls, 10 Potions, 10 Revives, 1 Incense	

8	7,000	28,000	15 Poké Balls, 10 Potions, 5 Revives, 10 Razz Berries, 1 Lure Module	Razz Berry
9	8,000	36,000	15 Poké Balls, 10 Potions, 5 Revives, 3 Razz Berries, 1 Lucky Egg	
10	9,000	45,000	15 Poké Balls, 10 Super Potions, 10 Revives, 10 Razz Berries, 1 Incense, 1 Lucky Egg, 1 Egg Incubator, 1 Lure Module	Super Potions
11	10,000	55,000	15 Poké Balls, 10 Super Potions, 3 Revives, 3 Razz Berries	
12	10,000	65,000	20 Great Balls, 10 Super Potions, 3 Revives, 3 Razz Berries	Great Balls
13	10,000	75,000	15 Great Balls, 10 Super Potions, 3 Revives, 3 Razz Berries	
14	10,000	85,000	15 Great Balls, 10 Super Potions, 3 Revives, 3 Razz Berries	
15	15,000	100,000	15 Great Balls, 20 Hyper Potions, 10 Revives, 10 Razz Berries, 1 Incense, 1 Lucky Egg, 1 Egg Incubator, 1 Lure Module	Hyper Potions
16	20,000	120,000	10 Great Balls, 10 Hyper Potions, 5 Revives, 5 Razz Berries	

17	20,000	140,000	10 Great Balls, 10 Hyper Potions, 5 Revives, 5 Razz Berries	
18	20,000	160,000	10 Great Balls, 10 Hyper Potions, 5 Revives, 5 Razz Berries	
19	25,000	185,000	10 Great Balls, 10 Hyper Potions, 5 Revives, 5 Razz Berries	
20	25,000	210,000	20 Ultra Balls, 20 Hyper Potions, 20 Revives, 20 Razz Berry, 2 Incense, 2 Lucky Eggs, 2 Egg Incubators, 2 Lure Modules	Ultra Balls
21	50,000	260,000	10 Ultra Balls, 10 Hyper Potions, 10 Revives, 10 Razz Berries	
22	75,000	335,000	10 Ultra Balls, 10 Hyper Potions, 10 Revives, 10 Razz Berries	
23	100,000	435,000	10 Ultra Balls, 10 Hyper Potions, 10 Revives, 10 Razz Berries	
24	125,000	560,000	10 Ultra Balls, 10 Hyper Potions, 10 Revives, 10 Razz Berries	
25	150,000	710,000	25 Ultra Balls, 20 Max Potions, 15 Revives, 15 Razz Berries, 1 Incense, 1 Lucky Egg, 1 Egg Incubator, 1 Lure Module	Max Potions

26	190,000	900,000	10 Ultra Balls, 15 Max Potions, 10 Revives, 15 Razz Berries	
27	200,000	1,100,000	10 Ultra Balls, 15 Max Potions, 10 Revives, 15 Razz Berries	
28	250,000	1,350,000	10 Ultra Balls, 15 Max Potions, 10 Revives, 15 Razz Berries	
29	300,000	1,650,000	10 Ultra Balls, 15 Max Potions, 10 Revives, 15 Razz Berries	
30	350,000	2,000,000	30 Ultra Balls, 20 Max Potions, 20 Max Revives, 20 Razz Berries, 3 Incense, 3 Lucky Eggs, 3 Egg Incubators, 3 Lure Modules	Max Revive
31	500,000	2,500,000	?	
32	500,000	3,000,000	?	
33	750,000	3,750,000	?	
34	1,000,000	4,750,000	?	
35	1,250,000	6,000,000	?	
36	1,500,000	7,500,000	?	
37	2,000,000	9,500,000	?	
38	2,500,000	12,000,000	?	
39	3,000,000	15,000,000	?	
40	5,000,000	20,000,000	?	

The hefty rewards at level 5 correspond to your new status as a team member with unlocked ability to trai and combat at Gyms.

The major bonus boost you receive at levels 20, 25, and 30 correspond to the major XP you need to rack ι to level up afterward. While it may seem like a lovely gift for your achievement, the game is really giving you the most basic tools you need to move ahead in the game and not give up. Starting at level 20, you're going to have to dedicate a lot of time to visiting lures, hatching Eggs, hitting up PokéStops, and training your Pokémon to move forward in the game.

Level up faster!

1 Catch more Pokémon using Incense, visiting a lure site, or going on a long walk.

2 Hold the Poké Ball down to shrink the size of the inner ring before throwing. The smaller the inner ring, the more XP you earn with a skill catch.

3 Catch a Pokémon you've never caught before for 100 XP bonus.

4 Visit an area with a lot of PokéStops and stick around, visiting each one over and over between cooldowns.

5 Catch a bunch of the easy Pokémon like Pidgey, Ratatta, and Weedle and evolve them.

6 Use an app like Yelp to find a hangout place that's also a PokéStop like a library or park and visit the stop every time it recharges.

7 Use a Lucky Egg to double your XP for evolving, hatching, catching, and Training.

8 Troll lures and PokéStops to max out your opportunities to get supplies and catch more Pokémon. They also award you XP for every spin.

9 Visit cities, tourist attractions, major shopping centers, and other highly populated areas to start catching new species of Pokémon to get more supplies and rack up quick Experience Points.

Whenever I am close to leveling up, I usually look for Pokémon that can evolve and level up its CP to the point that it is in my top six to eight strongest.
—Acop42

10 Place Eggs in Incubators and hatch them by walking the required distance. Earn more Incubators through leveling up to hatch more Eggs at once, or purchase Incubators within the app.

11 Hold your finger down on the Poké Ball and spin it before you throw it to throw a curveball to get extra XP.

12 Train at a friendly Gym—one that's already held by your team. Training at a friendly Gym gives you more XP without the damage of fighting at a powerful rival Gym.

13 Join a local online community on Facebook to find out where players have found rare catches or plan meetups with people you know to track as a group. When more players are playing in one place, the game will reward you with better hunting prospects!

Use Incense and a Lucky Egg at the same time. The Incense will help you catch more Pokémon and the Lucky Egg doubles the XP for each one you catch, so they work together. —TennisBrandon

As you level up, the game gets harder. Pokémon become harder to catch. If you're having trouble catching a high CP Pokémon who tends to dodge and make faces at you, resist the temptation to hand your phone over to a friend to make the catch . . . you'll need to build your battle skills as you level up!

As you level up, the Pokémon you meet in the wild become more powerful. If you're a level 24 master and you're hunting with a level 6 noob, you'll both encounter a Pidgey in the same place, but your Pidgey will be a lot more powerful.

An added bonus of being an experienced player: your green friend may find the Pokémon in front of him has a red ring, indicating a very difficult catch, while your high-level catch may only have an orange ring and be easier to catch.

How to earn more XP to level up faster

For some people, reaching level 40 is their ultimate goal. Others may be happy just tracking, catching, and collecting and not worrying about leveling up faster. If you are looking to level up quickly, here are some achievements that will help you:

- Evolving a Pokémon—500 XP

- Hatching a Pokémon—200 XP

- Visiting a PokéStop—50 XP

- Catching a New Pokémon—500 XP

- Catching a Pokémon—100 XP

- Training at a friendly Gym—varies
  (see the chapter on training)

- Battling at a rival Gym—varies
  (see the chapter on battling for more info)

Tip: How to gain 30,000 XP in thirty minutes

Step 1: Catch lots of Pidgeys, catch lots of Weedles, and catch lots of Caterpies. Since these three are the most common Pokémon to find anywhere and each only require 12 Candies to evolve, they're the easiest to stockpile. You'll need about 10 × 12 Candies of each type, or 120 Pidgey Candies, 120 Weedle Candies, and 120 Caterpie Candies as well as 10 of each type you want to evolve. Earn more Candies by trading any more than 10 Pokémon of that type with Professor Willow.

Step 2: Make sure you have a Lucky Egg. A Lucky Egg will double all the XP you earn for a half hour!

Step 3: Get comfortable, activate that Lucky Egg, and start evolving your Pidgeys, Caterpies, and Weedles as quickly as you can. Each evolution normally earns 500 XP—or 1000 XP if you've never evolved that type of Pokémon before—but with a Lucky Egg, you'll double that for a whopping 1000 XP for every evolution. At one evolution a minute, you'll earn 30,000 XP and level up at least once to level 20, and potentially increase a few levels if you're just starting out in the early stages of game play.

10

GYM TRAINING TIPS & TRICKS

If you're a seasoned Pokémon video game aficionado, you're used to turn-based play as you wander the world going about your business. In Pokémon GO, battles are only stationed at Gyms. Niantic has hinted that they might add a system that allows people to battle outside of Gyms. You can pit your Pokémon against a computer-controlled NPC (non-player character) to enter a timed battle that lasts 100 seconds.

While you could play the game and never enter a Gym Battle, you would be missing out on a big part of game play if you didn't at least dip your toe into the pond of Gym training. You'd also be missing out on collecting a lot of what you'll need to level up, get better Pokémon, and earn more rewards.

Gym Battles are based on HP and CP—Hit Points and

Combat Power. A Pokémon's Hit Points tell you how much damage your Pokémon can receive in battle. All Pokémon lose HP when hit in battle, and if a Pokémon loses all of its HP, it will faint.

TIP: Tag A Pokémon

If you find your Pokémon is running low on HP, you can tag in another Pokémon in its place using the buttons at the bottom of your screen.

A Pokémon's Combat Power tells you how strong your Pokémon will be in battle. Each species of Pokémon has a set maximum CP value, and while the actual amount of starting CP your Pokémon has when you catch or hatch it is sort of random, it is affected by your Trainer level at the time the Pokémon is acquired. Each Pokémon has its own attacks as well, and not all Pokémon of the same type have the same attack powers.

GYM BASICS

Gyms are stationed at fixed locations. They are usually placed at active locations such as sporting arenas, actual gyms, fire houses, police stations, public parks, and big open spaces that encourage activity. They can also be found at gathering places like monuments, museums, libraries, and public art spaces.

A claimed Gym will show up on your map topped with a monument featuring the most powerful Pokémon defending that Gym as well as the color of the team that has control of the Gym.

An unclaimed Gym tower will appear white. Unclaimed Gyms are not currently controlled by any team and can be claimed for a team by placing a Pokémon to defend it.

When a Gym appears on your map, you can click on it for a closer look, even if you're not close enough to activate it, as long as you've passed level 5 and picked a team. If you're not on a team yet, you will be instructed to come back when you've reached level 5.

If you've reached level 5 but haven't picked a team yet, you'll be offered an opportunity to select your team when you click on the Gym.

Clicking on a claimed Gym when you're on a team will open the Gym screen. Swipe through the list of defenders to see which players have placed a Pokémon to defend the Gym as well as details about the Pokémon they have placed. The most powerful Pokémon will be displayed first, marked with a crown to show they are the prime defender, and they will go down in decreasing order of CP.

If a Gym is currently being challenged, the Map View of the tower will show explosions and battle signs.

Each defender screen will display

1 The name (or nickname) and image of the Pokémon placed at the Gym

2 Its CP

3 The Trainer name, avatar, and level

4 The Gym's level, Prestige, and Gym name

5 A photo of the real world Gym location

Why click on a Gym at all?

To help pick a team, some players check their neighborhood Gyms to see which team is in control and which teams are weak in terms of defense. Depending on the type of player you are, you can either select the most powerful team or the team that needs the most help.

- Click on Gyms in your area to see if your friends are defending any Gyms and check on their progress.

- Click on a rival Gym to see how powerful its defenses are. If you have more powerful Pokémon in your Pokédex, you can send in a Pokémon to do battle in an attempt to lower the Gym's Prestige and take over the Gym for your team.

- Click on a Gym held by your team to train your Pokémon and help defend the Gym for your team. Training your Pokémon gives you more XP and increases your Gym's Prestige.

- Claim a Gym and hold it for a whole day to earn a Defender Bonus, which gets you lots of PokéCoins.

GYM TRAINING

Visit a friendly Gym to increase your team's Prestige Points and make it harder to lose control of the Gym.

Visit a rival Gym to chip away at another team's Prestige and bring you one step closer to conquering the Gym for your own team.

Visit a neutral Gym to claim it for your team. Leave a Pokémon behind to defend the Gym for your team.

When you train, your most powerful Pokémon will be selected from your inventory to battle against each defending Pokémon in sequence. Each time you win, you earn 50 XP for yourself and more Prestige for your team.

To join a friendly battle, click on the Gym to enter, then click the boxing glove on the lower right corner. The Pokémon with the highest CP will automatically be drawn into battle with each of the defending Pokémon at the Gym, starting with the defending opponent who has the lowest CP. You'll keep battling until either your Pokémon loses all HP and faints or you beat all of the Gym's defenders.

You can always use Potions to restore your strongest Pokémon's health and place it in a defeated Gym.

Placing a Pokémon can be tricky, because you can't use that Pokémon while it's defending a Gym. I usually choose my second or third best. It's important to choose a Pokémon with few weaknesses or those with hard-to-find weaknesses such as psychic types. Bugs are really underused while dark and ghost types have weaknesses that are easier to exploit. —DroptheSammer

After each battle, check on your Pokémon to see its current health. The line below the Pokémon's image will be filled with blue if it is at full health, or grayed out when it's in need of healing. Whether you win or lose, it's bound to have lost some HP.

When your Pokémon faints in a friendly Training battle, it will be returned to your collection at 1HP and will need to be refreshed with one or more sprays of Potion, depending on the amount of HP that needs to be restored.

When a Pokémon faints while claiming a Gym, it will lose all of its HP and need to be fully revived using a Revive from the Items.

To restore HP to a battle-weary Pokémon, open the main menu by clicking on the Poké Ball, then click on your Items on the bottom right. Click on the Potion in your inventory to pull up a list of all of the Pokémon who are in need of healing. Click the Pokémon to be healed. For each click, you use up one draught of Potion to restore the HP of your Pokémon by 20 points. To fully restore a Pokémon, you may need to use more than one spray. A heart will appear next to your Pokémon to show its health has been restored.

If you have no Pokémon in need of healing, the Potion menu will not list any Pokémon. Close out the menu and head over to another battle or training session.

PRESTIGE—WHAT IT IS AND HOW TO GET MORE OF IT FOR YOUR TEAM

Each time you train in your team's Gym, you earn Prestige Points for the Gym. When it reaches a certain number of points, the Gym levels up and can hold more defenders. More defenders make it harder for other teams to capture a Gym.

A Gym can hold up to ten defenders and have a maximum of 50,000 Prestige Points.

Claiming a Gym

If you're lucky enough to find a neutral Gym and place a Pokémon of your own to defend it, you have claimed the Gym for your team. While you can only place one Pokémon at any Gym to defend it, your friends and neighbors on the same team can add their Pokémon to improve your Gym's defense. The Pokémon with the highest CP is noted with a red crown.

The most unusual Gym I've seen is about thirty feet away from the line for platform 9 ¾ at King's Cross Station in London. —Acop42

CARA COPPERMAN

Challenging a Gym

You can approach a Gym held by another team and challenge their dominance of that Gym. Each successful challenge lowers the Gym's Prestige and brings you one step closer to wresting control away from that team. Be careful to stay within range of the Gym when battling or the fight will end and not count.

In a Gym challenge, you can select up to six of your own Pokémon, selecting them one by one or selecting them in a random shuffle. If the defending Pokémon are at a very high level, it's recommended to hand-pick your challengers based on the types of Pokémon guarding the Gym. You'll have to defeat all of the Pokémon defending the Gym, starting with the ones that have the lowest CP.

Check out the competition by scrolling through the list of the Gym's defenders before you choose your Pokémon to send into battle. Match them by CP and also by the Pokémon type. For example, if there are fire Pokémon guarding the Gym, send in your water Pokémon to take them down. Hand-pick your team like you're selecting an elite fighting force—one that works off of each other's strengths and weaknesses.

Click GO when you're ready to start.

You'll need to fight well, making all of their Pokémon faint or lose their round, in order to win the Gym Battle. Winning against the defending team decreases the Gym's Prestige. It also earns you 50 XP for every

Pokémon you defeat. If all of your Pokémon faint, you'll need to head back to the drawing board, heal your Pokémon with Potion, or Revive from your Items.

Once you defeat one Pokémon, your next battle will start instantly.

When fighting at a rival Gym, if your Pokémon's health is starting to fade, swap it out with a fresh Pokémon. Just tap on the swap button on the Gym screen to select from the other five Pokémon you brought into battle, then tapping on the one you want in that slot. This is not possible at a friendly Gym, where you can only bring one Pokémon into battle with you, however if it looks like you're fighting a losing battle, it's okay to retreat. Simply click on the WALK icon in the corner of the screen to exit the battle. Then you can heal your Pokémon with Potion and Power-Up your Pokémon for a rematch or find a Gym more suited to your level.

Because the Pokémon controlling the Gym are NPC— non-player characters whose fighting moves are controlled by the computer—you and your friends can all challenge the same Gym at the same time to bring down a Gym more quickly.

I don't have a strategy per se, if I have time to take over a Gym I will, but if it's my team's Gym already and there is room, I will always jump in.
—Wcpedorc

When you defeat a Gym, your team doesn't automatically take it over. Each win against a rival Gym takes down its Prestige. When the Prestige is completely erased, the Gym will become neutral and will be ready for you to take it over for your team.

Once a Gym turns gray, meaning it's neutral and up for grabs, seize the opportunity to control it for your team! Most Gyms don't stay neutral for long.

TIP: Defend Your Gym

If you've just taken over a Gym with a friend on the same team and no one else is around, defend it with a low CP Pokémon so your friend can easily defeat it and raise your Gym's Prestige.

Karping—Join the movement

Poor Magikarp has long been the joke of Pokémon players. This Pokémon is relatively powerless in any battle. Even its animated avatar shows it flopping helplessly on the ground.

But Pokémon GO players around the world have been giving Magikarp a nod, taking over Gyms then placing our floppy friend in charge. Whether it's just to be funny or to thumb your nose at the opposing team you've just dethroned in the name of your team, Magikarp's reign will rarely last long, but it's fun while it lasts!

DEFENDING YOUR GYM

If a spot is available at a Gym, the Add icon will appear—the icon looks like a Pokémon icon with a plus sign on it. Click the Add icon and select your second- or third-best Pokémon to leave at the Gym. Don't pick your best—it will remain at the Gym until it's defeated and you won't be able to take it with you into battle as you challenge rival Gyms to take down their Prestige Points and take over their Gyms.

Whether you claim a Gym or add your Pokémon to the list of defenders, defending a Gym requires more luck than actual skill for the simple reason that once you set up a Pokémon as a defender, the game's AI—artificial intelligence—takes over your battle moves when it comes up against any challengers. While this takes away the fun of head-to-head play against real players, it makes sense since you can place up to 10 Pokémon at different Gyms at the same time, and you won't be sticking around to see who challenges your Pokémon for the next twenty-one hours.

Reasons why you may be having trouble placing your Pokémon in a Gym

1 You haven't reached level 5 or chosen a team yet. Grab a few more XP and come back when you've reached level 5.

2 Your Pokémon does not have full HP—a Pokémon must have all of its health points to be placed in a Gym. Restore your Pokémon's health using Potion or Revive, then try again.

3 The Gym has too many people guarding it already. A Gym can only have a limited number of defenders. The number is based on the Prestige level of the Gym. To increase the Gym's Prestige, have a friendly battle against your teammates defending the Gym. When the Gym levels up, you can pop your full HP Pokémon in and join the line of defense.

TIP: How to place

If you place one Pokémon, you might as well place a lot of Pokémon at several Gyms to increase your Defender Bonus.

Earning a Defender Bonus

When you leave your Pokémon to defend a Gym, you have the potential to earn PokéCoins (in-game currency you can use in the shop) and Stardust, which you can use to make your Pokémon stronger. If your Pokémon hasn't been kicked out and stays at a Gym for twenty-one hours, you receive a Defender Bonus.

To claim your Defender Bonus, visit the shop and click on the Shield icon in the top right corner. Once you claim it, you receive 500 Stardust and 10 PokéCoins. If your team loses control of the Gym, the timer won't reset—you still have a chance to take back the Gym in order to get your bonus.

TIP: Make sure you claim your bonus as soon as it's ready. The clock won't reset to start the next twenty-one hours until you claim it.

The Defender Bonus is the only way to get PokéCoins without paying for them.

Godefridus's top Gym tips

Godefridus is a level 25 Pokémon GO player who is not only a huge Pokémon fan, he's also a competitive Pokémon video game veteran. "I've been a Pokémon fan since the beginning even though their games have become rather repetitive," he says. "I'm glad they finally came out with this new concept. I dedicate around four or five hours a day to leveling up/playing. I used to play solo but I met new friends while playing and now I play with them every day."

- Look for areas that aren't as populated (for example in Garwood, NJ [population 4,300], I held a Gym for five days).

- The best times to capture Gyms is either early morning or really late past 2 A.M. because you're less likely to lose control of those Gyms immediately after capture.

- If possible you'll want friends on the same team to take down Gyms or train ally Gyms with you (it saves you a lot of time).

- Unfortunately not many players are in Team Instinct so I have to solo takeover a lot of Gyms. While it's not difficult, it's very tedious. It can take me up to thirty minutes to take down a high-level Gym by myself.

You usually want to put your second strongest Pokémon in every Gym you takeover until the final Gym which is where you put your strongest.

If you're in a team group, at least one teammate should put in a fairly weak Pokémon so that it's easier for everyone to train up the Prestige of a Gym.

When attacking a Gym if their Pokémon are much lower CP than yours, just rapidly tap your screen without bothering to dodge and using your second attack when convenient.

If your opponent has an incredibly strong defense, try to dodge big attacks when possible.

BATTLE STATIONS

THE ART OF WAR: HOW TO FIGHT A POKÉMON GYM BATTLE

The mechanics are pretty simple, and usually involve little more than a lot of tapping and swiping to attack and dodge your opponent's attacks.

Normal Attacks: Tap as quickly as possible to use your Pokémon's Normal Attack.

Special Attacks: When the blue bar beneath your Pokémon fills up, you can launch a Special Attack by holding your finger on the screen and pressing it.

TIP

Mind your Attack Meter. Watch it charge and wait to launch your attack. It recharges at about one-fifth per second, so it should recharge completely every five seconds.

Dodging: Swiping your finger immediately after the yellow flash during a battle animation can help you dodge an attack. A message will appear over your opponent's head right before it uses its Special Attack, so be prepared to swipe and dodge to avoid getting hit.

GETTING TO KNOW YOUR POKÉMON'S ATTACKS

When you click on a Pokémon in your menu, scroll down to see its special combat moves. The first move listed is its Normal Attack that it performs when you tap repeatedly. The second move listed is its Special Attack. The lines next to the Special Attack represent the amount of the Attack Meter that is used up on a single attack. Several shorter dashes use up less of the Attack Meter with each attack, meaning you can use the Special Attack more times between recharging. One long dash indicates that the Special Attack is more powerful but also takes up more of the charge, and it's important to remember that the Special Attack can only be used when the Attack Meter is charged. When you use the Special Attack, there is a cooldown period where your Pokémon needs to recharge and can't attack, so using the Special Attack will leave your Pokémon defenseless for a moment. On the flip side, if your opponent uses a Special Attack, they're fair game and you can hit them quickly while they recharge.

When you're looking at a Pokémon's Normal and Special Attacks on their menu page, you'll notice that this is another important way Pokémon of the same type can differ greatly from each other.

EXAMPLES

You can have an Eevee with a Normal Quick Attack that deals 10 damage and a Special Ground Dig Attack that deals 70, while you can have another Eevee with the same Normal Attack but a Special Body Slam Attack that deals 40.

Your 76CP Krabby can deal a Bubble Water Normal Attack with 25 damage and a Water Pulse Attack dealing 35 with 4 uses per charge, but your 154CP Krabby with almost double the CP hits an opponent with a Ground Mud Shot dealing only 6 damage and a Vice Grip Special Attack dealing 25 with 5 uses per charge.

Choosing the right Pokémon for the job

All things being relatively equal, the Pokémon with the higher CP *should* win, but that is where choosing your battles and developing a strategy come into play.

CHOOSING BY POKÉMON TYPE

If you're up on your Pokémon battle strategy from other games, you'll know there is a fairly circular order of operations to Pokémon strengths and weaknesses very similar to rock-paper-scissors: Paper covers rock, rock smashes scissors, scissors cut paper.

In Pokémon, fire beats grass, grass beats water, and water beats fire. That means a water defense type will do more damage against a fire Pokémon and less damage against a grass type Pokémon. But with eighteen types, it gets a little more complicated. When you're ready to take over a Gym, check out the competition by clicking on the Gym and scrolling through the list of defenders, noting the type of each Pokémon. Then check the chart below to see which Pokémon type will work best—and worst—against your opponents. Once you know what you're up against, select the best Pokémon for each job and form your SWAT team. For your first few battles, it helps to write down which Pokémon you'll use against which opponents, or at least put your Pokémon in order so you'll be ready in the heat of the battle.

When selecting your Pokémon, note the types of attack your Pokémon has. Most Pokémon attacks are true to their type—water type Pokémon usually have water attack. However not all Pokémon attacks match their types. The Gastly Pokémon that I just caught while writing this sentence, for example, has a Dark Normal Attack and a Dark Special Attack. You can just as easily get a water type Krabby with a Mud Shot Ground Attack as a Bubble Water Attack, so check the attack types as well as your Pokémon types for a good true matchup, especially when you're fighting at 1,000CP and above.

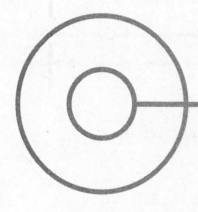

For each Pokémon type listed below, the first line lists what types the offensive mood is effective against. The second line lists what types can overpower it.

Bug

Bug types in Pokémon GO: Beedrill, Butterfree, Caterpie, Kakuna, Metapod, Paras, Parasect, Pinsir, Scyther, Venomoth, Venonat, and Weedle

1. Beats: Grass, Psychic, Dark

2. Gets beaten by: Fire, Flying, Rock

Dark

Dark types in Pokémon GO: None

1. Beats: Psychic, Ghost

2. Gets beaten by: Fighting, Bug, Fairy

Dragon

Dragon types in Pokémon GO: Dragonair, Dragonite, and Dratini

1 Beats: Dragon

2 Gets beaten by: Ice, Dragon, Fairy

Electric

Electric types in Pokémon GO: Electabuzz, Electrode, Magnemite, Magneton, Pikachu, Raichu, Voltorb, Jolteon, and Zapdos

1 Beats: Water, Flying

2 Gets beaten by: Ground

Fairy

Fairy types in Pokémon GO: Clefairy, Clefable, Jigglypuff, Mr. Mime, and Wigglytuff

1 Beats: Fighting, Dragon, Dark

2 Gets beaten by: Poison, Steel

Fighting

Fighting types in Pokémon GO: Hitmonchan, Hitmonlee, Machamp, Machoke, Machop, Mankey, Poliwrath, and Primeape

1 Beats: Normal, Ice, Rock, Dark, Steel

2 Gets beaten by: Flying, Psychic, Fairy

Fire

Fire types in Pokémon GO: Arcanine, Charizard, Charmander, Charmeleon, Flareon, Growlithe, Magmar, Ninetales, Ponyta, Rapidash, and Vulpix

1 Beats: Steel, Bug, Ice, Grass

2 Gets beaten by: Rock, Water, Ground

Flying

Flying types in Pokémon GO: Aerodactyl, Articuno, Butterfree, Charizard, Dodrio, Doduo, Dragonite , Fearow, Golbat, Gyarados, Moltres, Pidgeot, Pidgeotto, Pidgey, Scyther, Spearow, Zapdos, and Zubat

1 Beats: Grass, Fighting, Bug

2 Gets beaten by: Electric, Ice, Rock

Ghost

Ghost types in Pokémon GO: Gastly, Gengar, and Haunter

1 Beats: Psychic, Ghost

2 Gets beaten by: Ghost, Dark

Grass

Grass types in Pokémon GO: Bellsprout, Bulbasaur, Exeggcute, Exeggutor, Gloom, Ivysaur, Oddish, Paras, Parasect, Tangela, Venusaur, Victreebell, Vileplume, and Weepinbell

1 Beats: Water, Ground, Rock

2 Gets beaten by: Fire, Ice, Poison, Flying, Bug

Ground

Ground types in Pokémon GO: Cubone, Diglett, Dugtrio, Onix, Geodude, Golem, Graveler, Marowak, Nidoking, Nidoqueen, Rhydon, Rhyhorn, Sandshrew, and Sandslash

1 Beats: Fire, Electric, Poison, Rock, Steel

2 Gets beaten by: Water, Grass, Ice

Ice

Ice types in Pokémon GO: Articuno, Cloyster, Dewgong, Jynx, and Lapras

1 Beats: Grass, Ground, Flying, Dragon

2 Gets beaten by: Fire, Fighting, Rock, Steel

Normal

Normal types in Pokémon GO: Chansey, Ditto, Dodrio, Doduo, Eevee, Farfetch'd, Fearow, Jigglypuff, Kangaskhan, Lickitung, Meowth, Persian, Pidgeot, Pidgeotto, Pidgey, Porygon, Raticate, Rattata, Snorlax, Spearow, Tauros, and Wigglytuff

1 Beats: None

2 Gets beaten by: Fighting

Poison

Poison types in Pokémon GO: Arbok, Beedrill, Bellsprout, Bulbasaur, Ekans, Gastly, Gengar, Gloom, Golbat, Grimer, Haunter, Ivysaur, Kakuna, Koffing, Muk, Nidoking, Nidoqueen, Nidoran (Female), Nidoran (Male), Nidorina, Nidorino, Oddish, Tentacool, Tentacruel, Venomoth, Venonat, Venusaur, Victreebel, Vileplume, Weedle, Weepinbel, Weezing, and Zubat

1 Beats: Grass, Fairy

2 Gets beaten by: Ground, Psychic

Psychic

Psychic types in Pokémon GO: Abra, Alakazam, Drowzee, Exeggcute, Exeggutor, Hypno, Jynx, Kadabra, Mr. Mime, Slowbro, and Slowpoke

1 Beats: Fighting, Poison

2 Gets beaten by: Bug, Ghost, Dark

Rock

Rock types in Pokémon GO: Aerodactyl, Geodude, Golem, Graveler, Kabuto, Kabutops Onix, Omanyte, Omastar, Rhydon, and Rhyhorn

1 Beats: Fire, Ice, Flying, Bug

2 Gets beaten by: Water, Grass, Fighting, Ground, Steel

Steel

Steel types in Pokémon GO: Magnemite and Magneton

1 Beats: Fairy, Ice, Rock, Steel

2 Gets beaten by: Electric, Fire, Steel, Water

Water

Water types in Pokémon GO: Blastoise, Cloyster, Dewgong, Goldeen, Golduck, Gyarados, Horsea, Kabuto, Kabutops, Kingler, Krabby, Lapras, Magikarp, Omanyte, Omastar, Poliwag, Poliwhirl, Poliwrath, Psyduck, Seadra, Seaking, Seel, Shellder, Slowbro, Slowpoke, Squirtle, Starmie, Staryu, Tentacool, Tentacruel, Vaporeon, and Wartortle

1 Beats: Fire, Ground, Rock

2 Gets beaten by: Electric, Grass

12

CARING FOR YOUR POKÉMON

Get to know your Pokémon

Have you noticed on your Pokémon screen that not all Pokémon of the same type are exactly the same? When you click on the menu button and click on the Pokémon tab on the left, you'll come to the Pokémon screen. Click on a Pokémon to learn more about what makes it special.

At the top, you'll see your Pokémon's current CP or Combat Points. These points can be increased with Stardust and Candy to make your Pokémon a stronger fighter. Your Pokémon's maximum potential CP increases as you level up as a Trainer. If you Power-Up your Pokémon to its maximum limit then reach another Trainer level later, you'll have more room to Power-Up your Pokémon again. When you start Powering-Up your Pokémon, you'll just need one Candy and a small amount of Stardust, but to get great power, you'll need to pay more—more Candy and Stardust will be required to Power-Up your Pokémon at higher levels.

Under your Pokémon's lovely animated portrait, you'll find its name, and below that its HP or Health Points. Your Pokémon will be at full HP (52/52 means 52 out of a possible 52, for example) if you've never used it to train, fight, or defend a Gym.

The next line gives you its stats: type (for example, if you have a Clefairy, the type would be Fairy), Weight, and Height. Just like any being you'll find out in the wild—even people—some Pokémon are average-sized, some are bigger, and some are smaller. In terms of fighting, power, or any other performance issues, an XS or XL next to your Pokémon's weight or height doesn't mean a thing. It's just a nice way to tell one Pokémon of a species from the next. There are even a few achievements—Youngster and Fisherman, to be exact—that are earned by catching XS versions of Rattata and Magikarp.

The next line down gives you Power-Up and Evolve options, where you can make your Pokémon stronger and battle-ready or evolve your Pokémon to its next, stronger phase. The buttons will be green when you're able to activate them and make your Pokémon stronger, or gray if you need to collect more resources first.

The Power-Up line indicates how much Stardust and how much Candy you'll need to increase your Pokémon's CP. As mentioned above, the maximum CP available for each Pokémon species increases as you level up as a Trainer, so even if you max out with a Power-Up at level 8, you'll be able to make your Pokémon even stronger later on in the game as your Pokémon's max CP threshold increases.

Health Points: How to heal and revive your Pokémon to fight another day

After each battle, click on your Pokémon from the main menu and check its health level. Chances are that it will be a little lower than full, even if you've won the battle. Every hit takes down your Pokémon's health a notch or two. The more powerful the opponent, the more powerful its strikes and the more it will take down your Pokémon's health.

If your Pokémon faints in a friendly Training battle at a Gym your team controls, it will be returned to your Pokédex at 1HP, even if its entire HP has been depleted.

To heal your Pokémon

1 Click on the Poké Ball to bring up the main menu.

2 Click the backpack or "Bag" icon to pull up your items.

3 If your Pokémon has 1 or more HP left, select the Potion icon.

4 Select the Pokémon you wish to heal. Note that only the injured Pokémon will appear for you to choose from. You can't heal a Pokémon that is already at full health.

5 A Potion will restore 20HP to your Pokémon. Most Pokémon you send into battle have a higher starting HP and will need more than one Potion application to heal them.

6 If your Pokémon has 0HP left, you'll need to revive it. Select Revive from the menu.

The Revive will bring the Pokémon back to life, but you will still need to give it one or more doses of Potion to heal it.

TIP: Collect Potions

Out of Potions or Revives? Wow—you must battle a LOT! Hop on your bike or head out for a walk to your favorite neighborhood cluster of PokéStops and hang around long enough to collect the Potions and Revives you need. Don't worry—your Pokémon will wait patiently until you have what you need to restore them back to full health! Remember, at higher levels you can get Super, Hyper, and Max Potions, too.

Everything you need to know about CP and HP

Before you reach level 5, you're not too concerned with the stats or power of your Pokémon in your collection. But every Pokémon has its own power stats attached to it, and that really comes into play once you start training and battling for control of Gyms. Some stats are common to every Pokémon of a certain type. Others are specific to the Pokémon you have in your collection. As you level up in the game, you'll come across more powerful Pokémon.

One big difference between Pokémon GO and other Pokémon games is that in Pokémon GO, Pokémon don't gain experience through battles. Instead, you Power-Up your Pokémon using Stardust and Candy.

We've already gone over how Candy can help your Pokémon evolve and grow stronger.

You can also increase the power of your Pokémon in several ways.

How to increase your Pokémon's CP

If you're a seasoned Pokémon player from before the days of Pokémon GO (does anyone even really remember life before this game?), you may be wondering where all the complicated stats are to determine your Pokémon's strength against another Pokémon in a battle. While, as you learned earlier, there is a rock-paper-scissors hierarchy where grass beats water, water beats fire, etc., the only stat that REALLY counts when you're battling a level 10 Gym against some beefed up Vaporeon Gym leader is CP or Combat Points. When you catch, hatch, or evolve a Pokémon, you get a snapshot if its status as a fighter. The CP bar gives you a sense of the maximum combat points it can get at your current Trainer level, and the CP number tells you how close you are to maxing out your Pokémon's true potential at that moment. Note that as you level up, so does your Pokémon's potential, so it can reach higher heights as you become better at what you do.

TIP: When To Level up

Don't waste your Stardust and Candies leveling up your Pokémon when you're at a low training level—below level 15, leveling up won't make enough of a dent because your Pokémon's CP maxes out at a low number. Instead, Power-Up your evolved Pokémon, which start out with higher CP potential and higher CP overall.

What you need to know about Stardust

You'll need Stardust to give your Pokémon a power boost, but it's not too hard to find. Every time you catch a new type of Pokémon, any time you hatch an Egg, any time you earn a Gym Defender Bonus, and every time you catch any Pokémon at all, you earn Stardust. You'll find as you start out in the game that you are racking up some serious Stardust but don't be tempted to spend it just because you have it. As mentioned above, Powering-Up before level 15 is pretty useless.

At the higher levels, powering up your Pokémon will also cost a lot more Stardust—you're running with the heavy hitters at the higher levels—so you'll be smart to save your Stardust until you're leveling up an already powerful Pokémon.

Here's How to Power-Up your Pokémon

1 Click to open the main menu Poké Ball.

2 Click on the Pokémon icon.

3 Select the Pokémon you want to Power-Up.

4 Select Power-Up.

If the Power-Up button is grayed out, you either don't have enough Stardust or you don't have enough Candy to give your Pokémon a boost. Check the numbers next to the Power-Up button showing how much you need and compare them to the numbers above the Power-Up button showing how much you have.

5 Check your Pokémon's stats to see how much power it gained to see if it's worth Powering-Up another Pokémon at your level or waiting to try again when you've leveled up as a Trainer.

COMPLETE POKÉMON GO POKÉDEX

This is a complete list of the Pokémon you can catch in Pokémon GO in the game's initial release.

Not all Pokémon can be caught in all locations. Regional Pokémon Mr. Mime, Tauros, Farfetch'd, and Kangaskhan can only be caught in certain locations, but they can be hatched from anywhere.

1.	Bulbasaur (Grass / Poison)
2.	Ivysaur (Grass / Poison)
3.	Venusaur (Grass / Poison)
4.	Charmander (Fire)
5.	Charmeleon (Fire)
6.	Charizard (Fire / Flying)

7. Squirtle (Water)
8. Wartortle (Water)
9. Blastoise (Water)
10. Caterpie (Bug)
11. Metapod (Bug)
12. Butterfree (Bug / Flying)
13. Weedle (Bug / Poison)
14. Kakuna (Bug / Poison)
15. Beedrill (Bug / Poison)
16. Pidgey (Normal / Flying)
17. Pidgeotto (Normal / Flying)
18. Pidgeot (Normal / Flying)
19. Rattata (Normal)
20. Raticate (Normal)
21. Spearow (Normal / Flying)
22. Fearow (Normal / Flying)
23. Ekans (Poison)
24. Arbok (Poison)
25. Pikachu (Electric)
26. Raichu (Electric)
27. Sandshrew (Ground)
28. Sandslash (Ground)
29. Nidoran (Female) (Poison)
30. Nidorina (Poison)
31. Nidoqueen (Poison / Ground)
32. Nidoran (Male) (Poison)

33. Nidorino (Poison)

34. Nidoking (Poison / Ground)

35. Clefairy (Fairy)

36. Clefable (Fairy)

37. Vulpix (Fire)

38. Ninetales (Fire)

39. Jigglypuff (Normal / Fairy)

40. Wigglytuff (Normal / Fairy)

41. Zubat (Poison / Flying)

42. Golbat (Poison / Flying)

43. Oddish (Grass / Poison)

44. Gloom (Grass / Poison)

45. Vileplume (Grass / Poison)

46. Paras (Bug / Grass)

47. Parasect (Bug / Grass)

48. Venonat (Bug / Poison)

49. Venomoth (Bug / Poison)

50. Diglett (Ground)

51. Dugtrio (Ground)

52. Meowth (Normal)

53. Persian (Normal)

54. Psyduck (Water)

55. Golduck (Water)

56. Mankey (Fighting)

57. Primape (Fighting)

58. Growlithe (Fire)

59. Arcanine (Fire)
60. Poliwag (Water)
61. Poliwhirl (Water)
62. Poliwrath (Water / Fighting)
63. Abra (Psychic)
64. Kadabra (Psychic)
65. Alakazam (Psychic)
66. Machop (Fighting)
67. Machoke (Fighting)
68. Machamp (Fighting)
69. Bellsprout (Grass / Poison)
70. Weepinbell (Grass / Poison)
71. Victreebel (Grass / Poison)
72. Tentacool (Water / Poison)
73. Tentacruel (Water / Poison)
74. Geodude (Rock / Ground)
75. Graveler (Rock / Ground)
76. Golem (Rock / Ground)
77. Ponyta (Fire)
78. Rapidash (Fire)
79. Slowpoke (Water / Psychic)
80. Slowbro (Water / Psychic)
81. Magnemite (Electric / Steel)
82. Magneton (Electric / Steel)
83. Farfetch'd (Normal / Flying)
84. Doduo (Normal / Flying)

85. Dodrio (Normal / Flying)
86. Seel (Water)
87. Dewgong (Water / Ice)
88. Grimer (Poison)
89. Muk (Poison)
90. Shellder (Water)
91. Cloyster (Water / Ice)
92. Gastly (Ghost / Poison)
93. Haunter (Ghost / Poison)
94. Gengar (Ghost / Poison)
95. Onix (Rock / Ground)
96. Drowzee (Psychic)
97. Hypno (Psychic)
98. Krabby (Water)
99. Kingler (Water)
100. Voltorb (Electric)
101. Electrode (Electric)
102. Exeggcute (Grass / Psychic)
103. Exeggutor (Grass / Psychic)
104. Cubone (Ground)
105. Marowak (Ground)
106. Hitmonlee (Fighting)
107. Hitmonchan (Fighting)
108. Lickitung (Normal)
109. Koffing (Poison)
110. Weezing (Poison)

111. Rhyhorn (Ground / Rock)
112. Rhydon (Ground / Rock)
113. Chansey (Normal)
114. Tangela (Grass)
115. Kangaskhan (Normal)
116. Horesa (Water)
117. Seadra (Water)
118. Goldeen (Water)
119. Seaking (Water)
120. Staryu (Water)
121. Starmie (Water / Psychic)
122. Mr. Mime (Psychic / Fairy)
123. Scyther (Bug / Flying)
124. Jynx (Ice / Psychic)
125. Electabuzz (Electric)
126. Magmar (Fire)
127. Pinsir (Bug)
128. Tauros (Normal)
129. Magikarp (Water)
130. Gyarados (Water / Flying)
131. Lapras (Water / Ice)
132. Ditto (Normal)—NOT IN THE GAME

133. Eevee (Normal)
134. Vaporeon (Water)
135. Jolteon (Electric)
136. Flareon (Fire)
137. Porygon (Normal)
138. Omanyte (Rock / Water)
139. Omastar (Rock / Water)
140. Kobuto (Rock / Water)
141. Kabutops (Rock / Water)
142. Aerodactyl (Rock / Flying)
143. Snorlax (Normal)
144. Articuno (Ice / Fighting)—NOT IN THE GAME
145. Zapdos (Electric / Flying)—NOT IN THE GAME
146. Moltres (Fire / Flying)—NOT IN THE GAME
147. Dratini (Dragon)
148. Dragonair (Dragon)
149. Dragonite (Dragon / Flying)
150. Mewtwo (Psychic)—NOT IN THE GAME
151. Mew (Psychic)—NOT IN THE GAME

THE POKÉMON STORY (THE GAME BEHIND THE APP)

Pokébugs?

It all started with a childhood fascination with bugs. As a child, Satoshi Tajiri's hobby was catching bugs and insects. As he grew, so did his idea. What if he created a game out of catching and categorizing monsters just like you can capture and categorize bugs? The game Capsule Monsters was created—and was *almost* born. It wasn't an easy process to launch this new idea. Satoshi Tajiri pitched this idea along with Ken Sugimori and their company Game Freak to Nintendo several times but were rejected.

It wasn't until Satoshi teamed up with Shigeru Miyamoto, the founder of Nintendo's two largest franchises, Super Mario and The Legend of Zelda, that Nintendo finally decided to fund the project. Due to unforeseen trademark issues, they had to change the name of the project from Capsule Monsters to Pocket Monsters, or Pokémon.

But even then, it wasn't an easy road. The game needed a whole lot of tweaks to work properly, which nearly caused Game Freak to go bankrupt. All of the changes took time and money, and that created major problems for Game Freak. But they believed in the idea, so they persevered until they succeeded in releasing the first Pokémon games—Red and Green—on February 27, 1996, on Nintendo's Game Boy system.

Pokémon still wasn't a huge hit at first. Game sales started slow, but it gained steam as the word spread about how fun it was to catch, train, and trade these characters. In Japan, the popularity continued with the launch of Manga series, the first one entitled Pokémon Pocket Monsters by Kosaku Anakubo. This led to other Manga series and eventually anime throughout the remainder of the 1990s.

This excitement then led to the launch of the Pokémon Trading Card game in 1996, developed by the company Media Factory. Now players could play and interact with each other in real life rather than playing against NPC's on the Game Boy. There were initially 102 cards in 1996. Currently, the Pokédex goes up to 721!

#1 in the Pokédex is Grass/Poison type Bulbasaur

#721 is Vulcanion, a Fire/Water Mythical Pokémon

The birth of Pikachu

It later became a world-wide phenomenon, which sparked the launch of Pokémon Yellow, introducing the world to Pikachu! As Nintendo developed new game systems—both hand-held and console—Pokémon always went along for the ride. Nintendo 64's Voice Recognition game called "Hey You, Pikachu" allowed people to interact with this now famous character. In 1999, Game Boy Color released Pokémon Pinball. They even launched a racing game called Pokémon Dash for the Nintendo DS in late 2004 in Japan which then hit the streets in North America by March of 2005.

2006 marked the tenth anniversary of Pokémon, which saw the launch of a Pokémon Trading Figure Game. Although it was initially distributed in Europe, Southeast Asia, and Australia in 2006, it reached North America and Japan a bit later—in 2007.

Spin-offs have extend well beyond video games and game cards to movies, videos, and animated series, not to mention plush toys, clothes, costumes, and entire tournaments devoted to everything Pokémon— see video game champion Godefridus's story below. The first Pokémon movie, titled *Pokémon: The First Movie: Mewtwo Strikes Back* was released in Japan on July 18, 1998 and then released in the United States as a subtitled TV special. Since the first movie, countless new theatrical releases have come out, based on the original Pokémon, Advanced Generation, Diamond, and Pearl series, Best Wishes and XY series.

As with the Pokémon movie series, the animated series has also had a long running success—and is still going. The animated series is broadcast in over seventy-four countries and is available on Netflix. The series focuses on Ash Ketchum, a Pokémon Trainer from Pallet Town, who's main goal is to become a Pokémon master. The series is based on the Pokémon games, however has its own unique take and story lines.

POKÉMON TIMELINE

1996   The Pokémon Red and Green games were released in Japan

1998   Pokémon Red and Blue games hit America with 151 original Pokémon

1998   The Pokémon cartoon show was released

2011   Players had to work harder to "catch 'em all" with 649 Pokémon to catch

2016   As of July, 2016, 718 Pokémon filled the Pokédex. The cartoon show is still on the air. And classic versions of Pokémon Red and Blue became available for download on Nintendo DS for the twentieth anniversary.[*]

On July 6, 2016, Pokémon GO was released

[*] http://bulbapedia.bulbagarden.net/wiki/Pok%C3%A9mon_GO verified at App Store for iOS

From casual Trainer to Pokémon master: Godefridus's story

I watched the TV show as a kid. It was one of the few shows I watched at the time because I didn't have cable. I remember collecting a lot of Pokémon cards, too, but never understanding how to play the card game even to this day. I never had a Gameboy so I had to watch my friends play all the early Pokémon games and I remembered the envy I felt. It seemed really fun, too.

I didn't get my first Pokémon game until Pokémon Ruby came out for the Gameboy Advance. Since it was my first game, I played it religiously. Over 300 hours of playtime into that single game (not an exaggeration) and I learned everything there was to know about Pokémon, including IVs and EV training.

Eventually I moved on to the other Pokémon games, even the generations I missed. I wanted to show off to my classmates, take advantage of the knowledge I learned about the game, and become unbeatable in battles. Later I found out there were online battle simulators for Pokémon and that had rankings and everything.

Pokémon in Japanese translates to Pocket Monsters— literally monsters that can fit in your pocket!

I began to study every Pokémon and how they functioned competitively and learned even more. All the tiers, all the movesets, even combinations of teams. When I gave the ranked ladder a try, I realized how good I actually was. A lot of online battling is more than just having strong Pokémon, it's about having a tactical mind and outsmarting your opponents. I've always appreciated games like that. Eventually after plenty of research, I developed my unbeatable doubles trick room team for competitive Pokémon and started entering tournaments. It was a great time but it does get repetitive at some point, so I retired.

CARA COPPERMAN

GLOSSARY

Battle

When a player arrives at a Gym, that player can choose Pokémon of different types to fight against the Pokémon at that Gym. At friendly Gyms, you can train your Pokémon in battles. At rival Gyms, each rival Pokémon you defeat reduces the Gym's Prestige and potentially lowers the Gym's level; reduce the Gym's Prestige to zero to capture the Gym for your team

Combat Power (CP)

A measure of a Pokémon's attack strength, which determines how well it can perform in battle

Defender Bonus

A daily reward of Stardust and PokéCoins for defending a Gym, which can be claimed at the shop

Eggs

Items that can be found at PokéStops that will hatch into a Pokémon after you walk a specific distance while they are in an Incubator

Evolution

The process of using Candy to change a Pokémon into a higher level, more evolved species of Pokémon

Candy

Used to evolve Pokémon to higher levels and to strengthen Pokémon. Can be acquired by catching Pokémon, hatching Eggs, and transferring Pokémon to Professor Willow

Experience Points (XP)

How your advancement is measured, and what needs to be increased in order for you to advance to higher Trainer levels

Fainted Pokémon

A Pokémon faints when it has zero HP; it must be revived with Revive or Max Revive

Gyms

Locations where you can battle the Pokémon of rival teams, or train your Pokémon by battling against the Pokémon placed there by your own team

—Friendly Gyms are those belonging to your team

—Rival Gyms are those that have been claimed by other teams

—Open Gyms have not been claimed by any team

Health Points (HP)

The measure of a Pokémon's health; when this is zero, the Pokémon faints and you must use a Revive or Max Revive item to revive it

Incense

Attracts wild Pokémon to your location with its scent

Incubator

Holds an Egg, where it will hatch into a Pokémon as you walk

Lure Module

Attracts wild Pokémon to a PokéStop for a limited time

Lucky Egg

Used to double the amount of XP you earn in a certain amount of time

Medals

Awarded for an array of achievements

Poké Balls

Items used to capture wild Pokémon, they can be found at PokéStops and bought in the shop

Great Balls, Ultra Balls, and Master Balls are high-performance versions that have more strength to catch wild Pokémon

PokéCoins

Currency that Trainers can exchange for premium items in the shop; can also be purchased in the shop

Pokédex

All the Pokémon species a player has caught are here, along with information about them.

PokéStops

Locations where players can gather Poké Balls, Potions, and Eggs. They change shape when a player walks close enough, and can interact with you when you touch them and spin the Photo Disc to get items

Potions

Used to heal Pokémon and restore their HP (Hit Points)

Power-Up

To increase a Pokémon's CP and HP using Stardust and Candy

Prestige

Measure of a Gym's progress; earned when Pokémon train at the Gym, and an increase can advance the Gym to higher levels

Razz Berry

Makes wild Pokémon easier to catch when fed to them during an encounter

Stardust

Acquired by catching Pokémon, hatching Eggs, and earning the Defender Bonus; used to Power-Up Pokémon

Training

At friendly Gyms, you can battle Pokémon assigned to that Gym by other members of your team to increase their XP and the Prestige of the Gym

Trainer

A Pokémon GO player

Wild Pokémon

Pokémon that have not been caught